Introduction

Ever since the start of Lambretta production, stories have circulated around many aspects of what is one of the world's most famous scooter brands ever. Anything from how each model was designed and built to how it was promoted to the public, leaving a trail of intrigue and mystery. Theories have built up among enthusiasts as to what happened at the factory in Milan and why, but it goes a lot further afield than that. The characters behind the Lambretta and those who promoted it all helped to create an even more incredible story.

More than 50 years have passed since the last one rolled off the production line and many of the tales persist. The problem is, as time marches on, they become ever more exaggerated and embellished in their retelling. This has resulted in much confusion, obscuring the truth from those who attempt to find out what really happened. Like any period in history, if you look hard enough, the facts are there no matter how deeply they might be hidden, and the Lambretta story has many of them.

This book aims to dispel some of those myths and reveal the truth about what actually occurred. Many stories can be explained by those who made them happen or by genuine documents that reveal the truth. Some tales and rumours are still unexplained, but hopefully this publication will jog the memories of those who can help solve the remaining Lambretta myths and legends.

PICTURE CREDITS
Andrew Stan Bates, Jimmy Dee, Darrell Milnes, Peter Nottingham, Dave Simpson, Stefan C. R. Smith, Tony Tessier, Steve Towers, Pierfranco Viviano, Michael Waters, Andy Weal, Gary Worsfold

Contents

Author: Stuart Owen
Design: Burda Druck India Pvt. Ltd.
Publisher: Steve O'Hara
Published by: Mortons Media Group Ltd, Media Centre, Morton Way, Horncastle, Lincol
Tel. 01507 529529

I0895436

ISBN: 978-1-911703-49-5

Section 1: Stories

1
The TV 200

Surely everyone would agree that the most exaggerated Lambretta story is that surrounding the TV 200 – everything from the reason it was created in the first place to how it got into production. If that wasn't enough, because it was an export model there were limited documents or physical evidence available from the Innocenti factory regarding it. The person who can give the honest answer is sadly no longer alive, but thankfully he was interviewed before his passing – providing a true insight into what happened. What he said must be taken as gospel and goes a long way to dispelling the myths surrounding it.

When Innocenti created the TV 175 series three, its groundbreaking and revolutionary front disc brake made it a first. No production two-wheeled vehicle in the world had ever had one fitted and Innocenti stunned everyone when they became the first to do so. With performance and styling to match, they saw no reason to try and better it, but that wasn't the same thinking elsewhere. The UK was in the grip of the motorway age during the 1960s, as it became the decade of opening up the country's road network nationwide. With long, vast stretches of uninterrupted tarmac and the speed limit being pushed up to 70mph, the automotive car industry responded by building faster and more powerful vehicles to suit it.

Lambretta Concessionaires had been hugely successful in the UK and was Innocenti's biggest customer, selling over a million machines in the process. Realising a more powerful Lambretta was now required, company boss Peter Agg insisted that a 200cc Lambretta be produced. While that was a perfectly acceptable request, he explained that Innocenti refused because, as far as they were concerned, there was no need for it. Peter was a successful businessman and wouldn't take no for an answer, so he persisted – with Innocenti finally giving in to his demands. It didn't come without specific terms however, to which he agreed, making some demands himself. Once this agreement was in place, things could get moving, taking the Lambretta in a new direction and, in so doing, creating many theories of how it had come about and what its design and manufacturing process had entailed.

Peter explained that Innocenti started by trying to modify the TV 175 cylinder, but there were problems with the bore being too thin because it was necessary to take it out to 66mm, meaning a seizure was more likely. Also, there was no marked improvement in performance so it wasn't worth the effort. Innocenti realised that the cylinder would need a bigger sleeve and a bigger inlet and transfer area to get the desired power. The only way to do this was by making a larger mouth on the crankcase to accept it and altering the four stud spacings to incorporate the more extensive port area.

Rather than create a new engine, something Peter mentioned they wouldn't do because of cost, a bigger mouth was cast onto the standard Lambretta casing. That meant it would accept the bigger cylinder, but everything else would remain the same. Once tested, the desired power improvement was gained, and around 50 prototypes were produced, but none came over to the UK and certainly not to the Lambretta Concessionaires factory. Peter also revealed that a 250 version was

The early version used the Li-type side panels but with two-tone paintwork and the much lower Pegasus seat

Innocenti did very little to promote it because it was an export model. Proof with this image in the instruction book, which is not of a TV 200 but a TV 175

PRESS RELEASE

Lambretta

Concessionaires Limited.

TROJAN WORKS · PURLEY WAY · CROYDON · SURREY
Telephone: MUNicipal 2499 (40 lines) Cables: Lambretta Croydon

Not for Publication Until
Thursday, May 9, 1963.

N E W 7 0 M. P. H. L A M B R E T T A 2 0 0 G. T. M O D E L

CUSTOM-BUILT EXCLUSIVELY FOR U.K. MARKET

"Most Significant Scooter Development For 10 Years"

Lambretta Concessionaires today (Thursday, May 9) announce an exciting addition to their scooter range: the Lambretta 200 G.T., a 198 c.c. 70 m.p.h., gran turismo model with polychromatic finish and acceleration akin to that of the E-type Jaguar.

It costs £199.17.6d (including £34.17.6d purchase tax) and is being built by Innocenti of Milan exclusively for the United Kingdom market.

"The introduction of this new high-performance Lambretta is the most significant scooter development for ten years" said Mr P. James Agg, Managing Director of Lambretta Concessionaires.

"The new 200 G.T. model, based on the Slimstyle 175, is custom-built for the U.K. to meet an insistent demand from scooter fans in two categories:

"(1) Those who want a livelier performance for competition work: and (2) Riders who use their scooters for long-range touring at fast cruising speeds.

"We are significantly adding the new 200 G.T to our existing Lambretta range at a time when the trend with other makes is towards smaller engines.

"The introduction of a more powerful Lambretta parallels the fashion, in the car world, for producing hotted-up versions of cars like the B.M.C. Minis with bigger engines and greatly improved performance to take full

The official UK press release from May 1963 announcing the new 70mph Lambretta GT 200 to the world

All UK press material listed it only as a GT 200

attempted, but it was felt that the 200cc offered the best choice of improved performance while still maintaining reliability.

The new model would be named the TV 200, which was a natural progression and would be an export-only model. That meant it didn't require homologation in Italy because it wouldn't be sold there. Consequently, it didn't require an IGM number, something Peter confirmed. He struck a deal with Innocenti that he would have sole rights to it in Europe and North America, meaning all TV 200s would be shipped to the UK first and dispatched to other countries from there. According to him, this agreement was only based on a handshake, but since Lambretta Concessionaires was Innocenti's biggest customer, they dared not renege on it. Towards the end of production, some were shipped to other countries directly from Italy but by this time it had proved such a success that Peter said he wasn't bothered about it. Just being vindicated in his decision to press for the 200cc Lambretta was enough for him.

Contrary to popular belief, the notion that Innocenti wouldn't supply it under warranty was, according to him, a load of rubbish. Indeed, the company didn't offer it for sale in its home territory, believing that if there were problems with it, it would be best if these happened on foreign soil. In reality, the only real problem was

The script badge on the front leg shields was TV 200

the silencer tail pipe snapping off and the right-hand side panel splitting due to increased vibration. Extra support was added to both, solving the problem, but Peter insisted that Innocenti shoulder the expense and provide a full warranty on the TV 200.

The other central myth surrounding the TV 200 was its branding, and because Peter Agg had the rights to the TV 200, he had control over that. At the time, as

TV 200 was also used on the rear frame badge inscription

cars were becoming faster, the term GT was frequently used, so he branded it the GT 200. All advertising, press releases and references were to the GT 200 – as was the log book supplied to owners with the scooter. But the machine itself remained badged as a TV 200 throughout its entire production and never deviated from this. Purists believe that to have an actual GT 200, it must have been registered in the UK originally, and imports that came in after production are not true examples. Regardless of what is thought, the GT 200 is a brand name only, and no factory-supplied Lambretta was ever badged as such.

2
Grand Prix 150 Electronic

By 1968, Innocenti was well underway with developing a new model to replace the SX range. It would be called the DL or, as it was rebranded in the UK, the Grand Prix. Though the overall dimensions of the chassis would remain the same, it was lowered at the front slightly by shortening the fork stem. Bertone's clever styling made the Lambretta look more modern without altering its overall shape. The engine also used the previous layout, but improvements were made to several components, the most significant being the crankshaft, which now featured a wider taper on the flywheel side. This was required because of the extra power on the 200cc model, which increased to 11.74bhp.

Homologation was approved for all models in October 1968, and all three variants would be launched at the beginning of 1969. Just over a year later, the Grand Prix 200 was offered with a new ignition system which would be controlled electronically. This would do away with the points and coil type system used on all previous models since production began in 1947. Ducati developed the system for their motorcycles, but having been the leading supplier of Lambretta ignition systems for many years, an option was created for it to fit on the Lambretta.

The only alteration required for the frame was a bracket on the right-hand side behind the petrol tank to fit the CDI unit, which replaced the coil that sat on the opposite side of where it was mounted. Figures show Innocenti started producing the GP 200 Electronic in May 1970, even though it would not be offered in the UK for another nine months. By this time the company was in dire financial trouble, and in May 1971 it was taken over by British Leyland, who finished production of the Lambretta in its entirety that month. This meant that no precise figure for how many Electronics

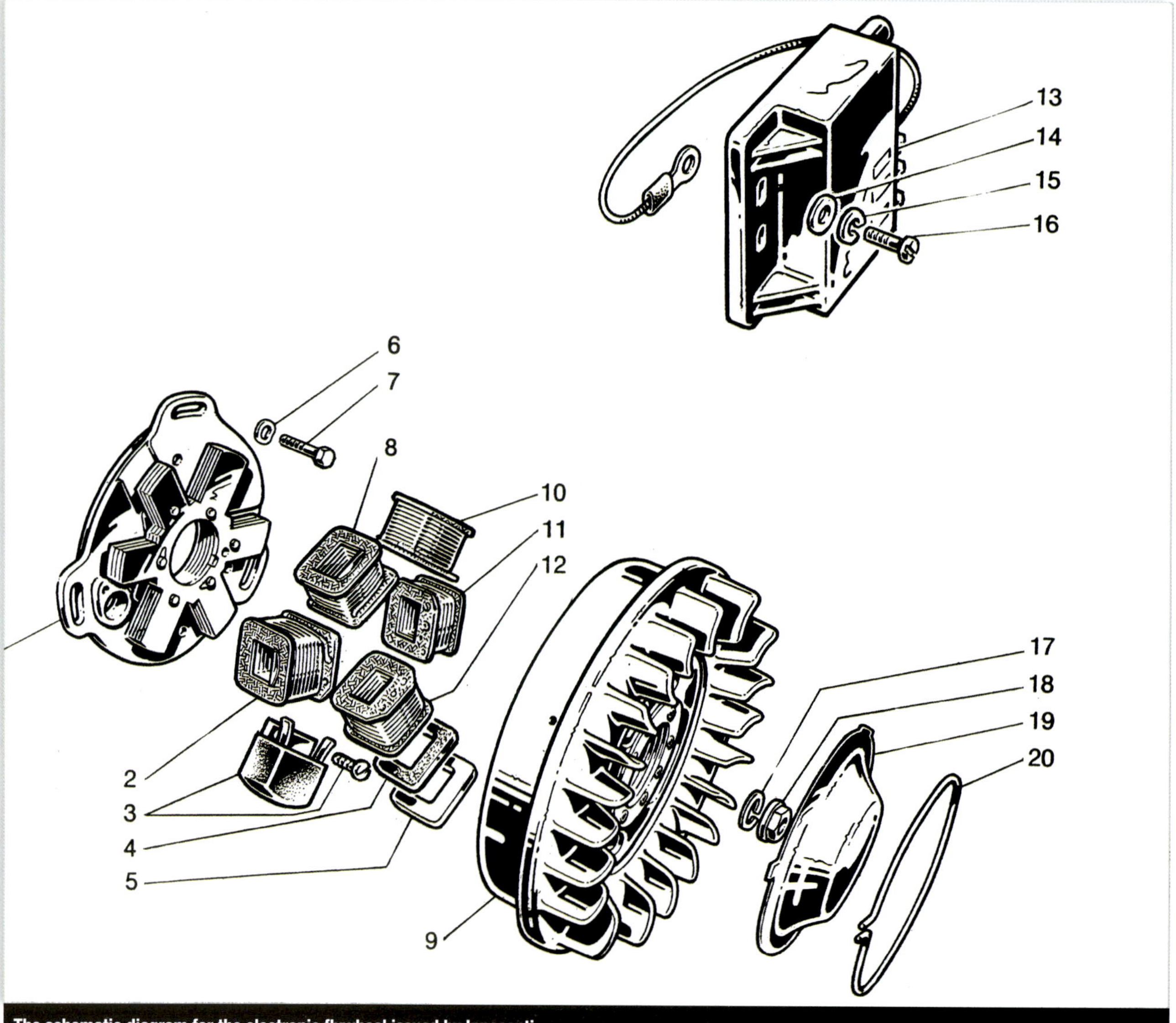

The schematic diagram for the electronic flywheel issued by Innocenti

The CDI coil mounting was on the left-hand side and spot-welded to the top shell support

Mese	PRODUZIONE MOTOVEICOLI 1970																			Totali
	MS non targati				Motor-scooters targati							Motofurgoni								
	50CL 50 S	50DL	50SP	Totale	75 S	75SL	125DL	150DL	200DL	200EL	Totale	500ML 175cc	500ML 200cc	550ML	600M	600V	550 Roma	Tri-lambr.	Totale	
Gennaio		1038		1038			588	1106	359		2053	3	354		314	544	30		1245	4336
Febbraio		1451		1451	59	10	569	925	561		2124	564	222		308	606	29		1729	5304
Marzo		1486		1486	32		493	953	529		2007	338	160	131	376	801	30		1836	5329
Aprile		719	929	1648	71		807	763	262		1903	334	132	172	411	858	30	9	1946	5497
Maggio	5	3	1360	1368			340	886	337	36	1599	202	36	256	215	910	30	1	1650	4617
Giugno			1449	1449			716	1125	112	191	2144	336	131	71	433	872	30	250	2123	5716
Luglio			1774	1774			829	799	167	32	1827	384	64	202	485	1070		500	2705	6306
Agosto			451	451			235	194	7	9	445	58		13	271	245			587	1483
Settembre		14	1773	1787	120		510	893	190	75	1788	216	76	12	556	626	60		1546	5121
Ottobre		50	1547	1597			455	556	300	103	1414	170	92	43	377	413			1095	4106
Novembre			1070	1070			537	778	175		1490	214	19	122	217	339			911	3471
Dicembre			1093	1093	240		401	509	135	250	1535	145	30	20	258	484			937	3565
Totali	5	4761	11446	16212	522	10	6480	9487	3134	696	20329	2964	1316	1042	4221	7768	239	760	18310	54851

The production figures for all Lambretta models in 1970 listed 696 GP 200 Electronics (highlighted in grey). There were no production figures issued for 1971 because production stopped in May of that year

Mod. D.G.M. 405

INNOCENTI
MILANO

★★ MOTOCICLO

Lambretta 150 dl (22/0)

Anno 1968

Aggiornato a ottobre 1969
•

Omologato dal Ministero dei Trasporti e dell'Aviazione Civile
Direz. Gen. Motorizz. Civile e T.C. Certificato n. 6437 OM in data 14-12-1968
E' autorizzato il rilascio della dichiarazione di conformità di cui all'art. 53 del T.U. 15-6-1959 n. 393

Le dimensioni relative ai dispositivi sono indicative. Per esigenze di fabbricazione sono ammesse piccole variazioni.

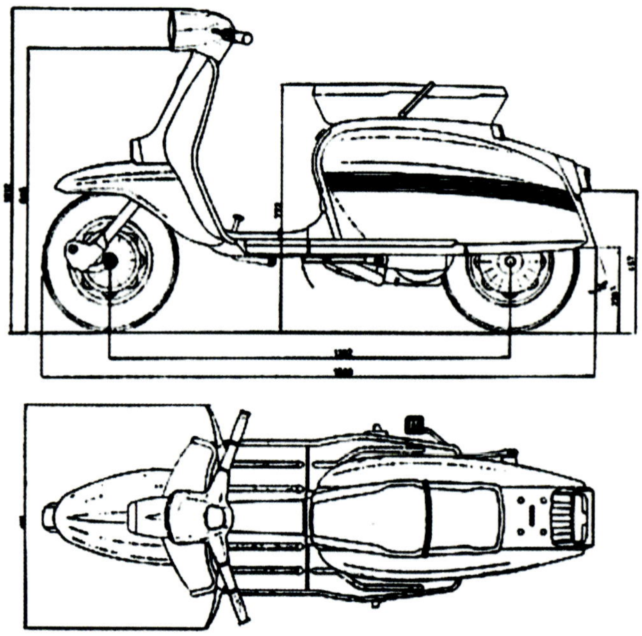

22/0 ✩ 0123456789 ✩
DGM.6437.OM

Punzonatura telaio: a destra sotto il serbatoio benzina effettuata su una sola riga.

★ **TIPO DELLA STRUTTURA:** telaio in tubi di acciaio e lamiera stampata, saldati

Posti	n°	2

DIMENSIONI

Lunghezza max	m	1,800
Larghezza max	m	0,680
★ Passo (a carico)	m	1,292
Diametro minimo di volta	m	3,30

PESI

Peso a vuoto kg 120 + conducente kg 70	kg	190
★ Peso complessivo (2 persone)	kg	280

SOSPENSIONI (tipo a descrizione)

anteriore: a biellette oscillanti e ruota tirata
posteriore: a molla elicoidale

RUOTE con cerchio 2.10

Pneumatici { anteriore 3.50 - 10
posteriore 3.50 - 10

★ **FRENI** (v. retro)

IMPIANTO ELETTRICO

Alternatore-magnete volano: volt 6 - watt 30 nomin.

Dispositivi illuminazione e segnalamento:

Proiettore con luce di posizione anteriore mutuamente incorporata, luce di posizione posteriore con luce di arresto mutuamente incorporata, luce di targa combinata con luce di posizione posteriore; catadiottro raggruppato con la luce di posizione posteriore; dispositivo di segnalazione acustica.

MOTORE:

★ Denominazione o Modello: SX 150
★ Funzionamento: ciclo Otto, miscela benzina-olio al 2%

★ Tempi	n°	2
★ Cilindri	n°	1
★ Diametro	mm	57
★ Corsa	mm	58
★ Cilindrata	cm³	148
Potenza fiscale	CV	3
Rapporto di compressione		1/7,8
★ Potenza max effettiva (I.G.M.)	CV	9,4
	a giri/min	6300

FRIZIONE a dischi multipli in bagno d'olio

CAMBIO DI VELOCITA' E TRASMISSIONE

N. 4 marce con comando a mano sulla manopola sinistra
Trasmissione primaria:

★ Motore-cambio: a catena	15/46 = 1/3,07
Cambio velocità: Prima	10/50 = 1/5,00
Seconda	12/42 = 1/3,50
Terza	15/39 = 1/2,60
Quarta	19/35 = 1/1,84

★ Velocità massima calcolata a n° giri di massima potenza (rapporto totale motore ruota: 1/5,65) km/h 86,3.

★ Ruota posteriore calettata sull'albero di uscita del cambio.

PRESTAZIONI:

1 km con partenza da fermo, solo pilota:
46,75 sec; 77 km/h

Velocità max effettiva, 1 km lanciato, solo pilota:
35,8 sec; 100,5 km/h

Velocità max effettiva, 1 km lanciato, pieno carico:
40,8 sec; 88,2 km/h

Consumo (norme CUNA) litri/100 km 3,28

SERBATOIO: Capacità totale litri 8,1

SILENZIATORE (v. retro)

★ Caratteristiche essenziali la cui modifica comporta la necessità di una nuova omologazione (art. 225 del D.P.R. 30-6-1959 n. 420).

The official homologation certificate released for the GP 150 in October 1968

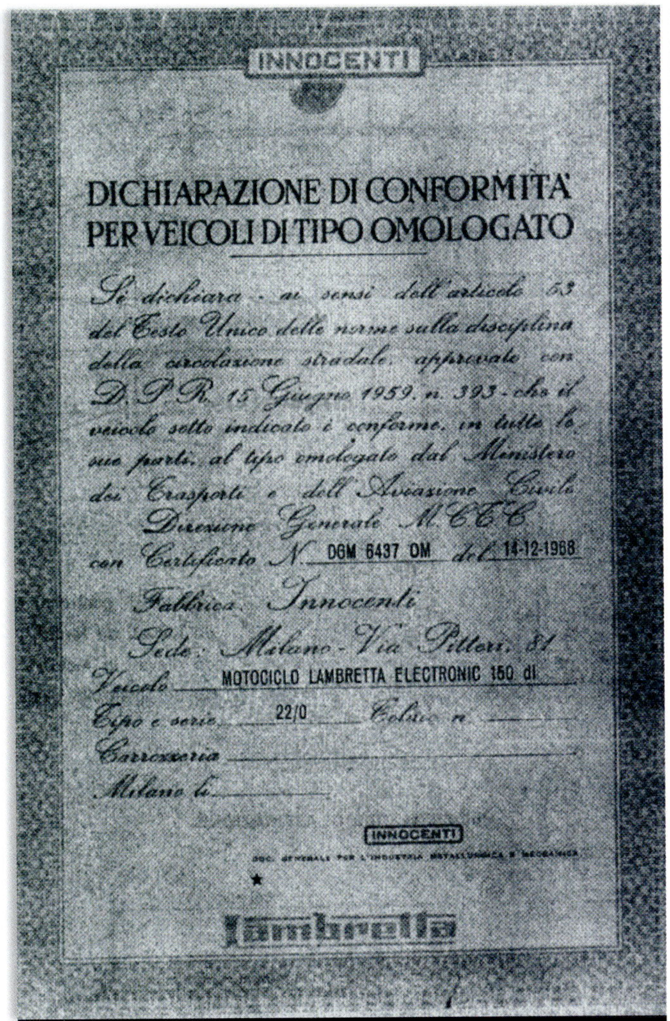

The certificate extension for the GP 150 Electronic dated 14 December 1968

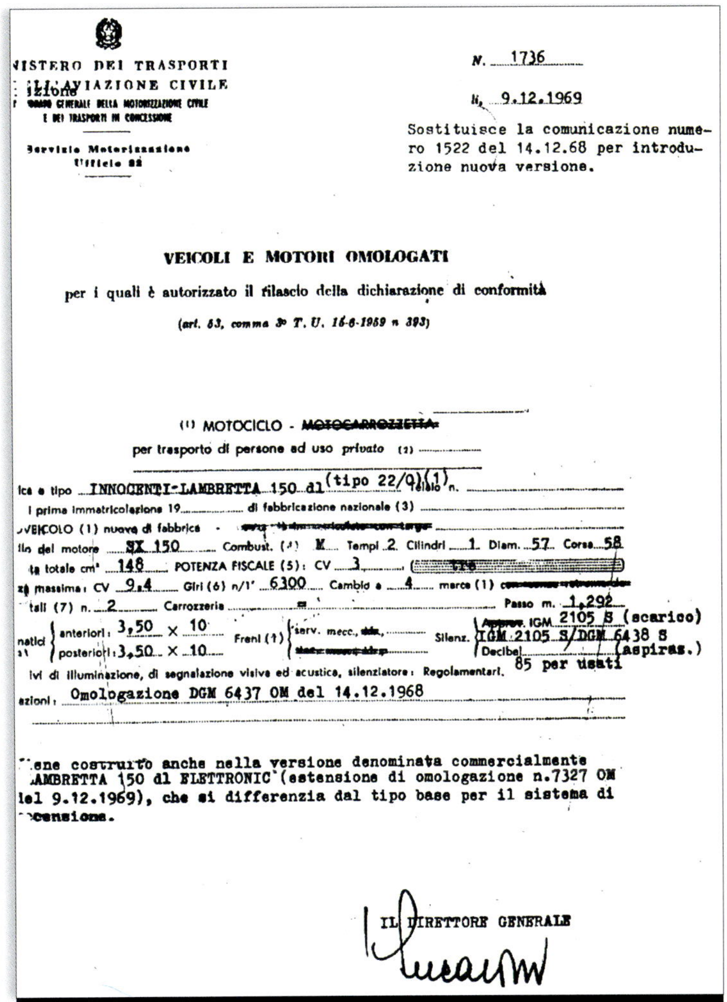

The second updated document from December 9, 1969 again mentions the GP 150 Electronic and shortly before the system appeared on the GP 200

were made was ever recorded, but it is believed to be around 1000. This has always been an accepted figure, but documents have now surfaced which question its accuracy.

On the homologation certificate for the GP 200, there is an extension paragraph in the description that states approval of the Electronic in December 1968, which means that the system was known about some 15 months before it went into production. What is more interesting and a legend surrounding the GP 150 is whether the electronic ignition system was fitted. Rumours have circulated for years that, in Italy, a few very late GP 150 frames were noted for having the CDI mounting bracket fitted. Those rumours as far as it went though – with no other evidence; it seemed as though anything was being done to keep production going during the last few months.

However, these rumours can now be verified because the homologation certificates that have surfaced for the GP 150 reveal an extension which states that full approval has been granted for it being fitted with electronic ignition. This now cements the evidence that the system was being made ready, even though Ducati may not have got it into production, appearing on the GP 200 over a year later. What it does prove is that it was also made available for the GP 150. While no evidence of one has been found, apart from the rumoured frames with the CDI brackets fitted, it doesn't mean one won't turn up in the future, and the existence of a GP 150 Electronic certainly cannot be ruled out.

3
What was Lambrettability?

Lambretta sales had peaked in the UK by 1960, though they remained solid, which meant Lambretta Concessionaires had many more good trading years in front of them. However, as the 1960s began, advertising coverage slowed down slightly. This was due to blanket coverage of the media and transport network in the 1950s as the company was establishing itself. As a recognised brand, there was no need to promote the Lambretta as much, but that didn't mean to say advertising would stop; it was just that the budget would be used more wisely.

At the height of series two production and with sales still strong, it became apparent that other manufacturers were directly copying the adverts put out by Lambretta Concessionaires. It infuriated company owner Peter Agg that other companies were benefitting from the money he had paid to those behind his advertising campaign – simply by slightly rewording their work.

He vented his anger at what he called "our vulnerable friends in the West" when referring to Douglas Bristol, where the Vespa was imported and built in the UK. He insisted the advertising agency come up with something that would be impossible for rivals to copy.

At the time, most of Lambretta Concessionaires' advertising work was farmed out to a company called Smee's in Sloan Square, London. A young up-and-coming advertising executive called Robert Wilkinson was in charge of the Lambretta account and he was tasked with delivering a new slogan that couldn't be copied without looking blatantly obvious.

His idea was to invent a new word – Lambrettability. He explained it was made up of the words Lambretta and mobility because of the freedom owning one allowed you. There was also a nod towards reliability, which Peter Agg wanted to get across; therefore, Lambrettability stood for several things. He was delighted with what Robert had created because it made the machine look good, and no other scooter manufacturer could copy it.

New adverts used the slogan immediately and this carried on for over a year before being changed. What Impressed Peter Agg was how quickly and easily Robert had devised the idea, and though it was simple, it made a huge impact. The clearly talented Robert was headhunted and offered a job by Lambretta Concessionaires, which he duly accepted. But strangely it wasn't in the advertising department. Instead, he was given the job of running the British Lambretta Owners Association (BLOA), which the company owned. However, over time, his skill at promoting BLOA was so evident that he was also given the job of running the advertising department.

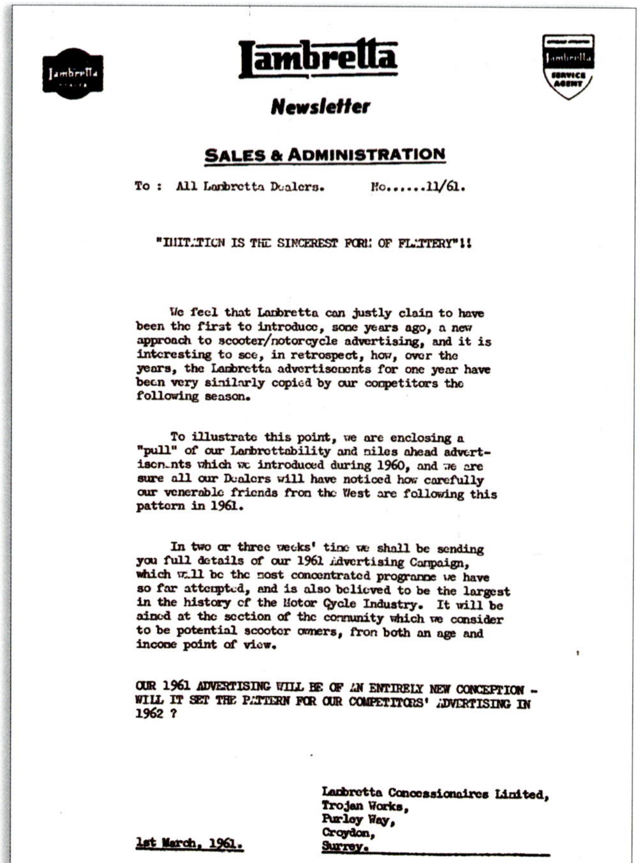
Lambretta

Newsletter

SALES & ADMINISTRATION

To : All Lambretta Dealers. No......11/61.

"IMITATION IS THE SINCEREST FORM OF FLATTERY"!!

We feel that Lambretta can justly claim to have been the first to introduce, some years ago, a new approach to scooter/motorcycle advertising, and it is interesting to see, in retrospect, how, over the years, the Lambretta advertisements for one year have been very similarly copied by our competitors the following season.

To illustrate this point, we are enclosing a "pull" of our Lambrettability and miles ahead advertisements which we introduced during 1960, and we are sure all our Dealers will have noticed how carefully our venerable friends from the West are following this pattern in 1961.

In two or three weeks' time we shall be sending you full details of our 1961 Advertising Campaign, which will be the most concentrated programme we have so far attempted, and is also believed to be the largest in the history of the Motor Cycle Industry. It will be aimed at the section of the community which we consider to be potential scooter owners, from both an age and income point of view.

OUR 1961 ADVERTISING WILL BE OF AN ENTIRELY NEW CONCEPTION - WILL IT SET THE PATTERN FOR OUR COMPETITORS' ADVERTISING IN 1962 ?

Lambretta Concessionaires Limited,
Trojan Works,
Purley Way,
Croydon,
Surrey.

1st March, 1961.

The press release from March 1961 announcing the Lambrettability advertising campaign

The draft advert attached to the press release shows dealers what it would look like

4
Was the Lambretta banned on motorways?

The scooter, in general, was initially intended as a local commuter vehicle and regarded as cheap, economical transport to mobilise the masses after the Second World War. That statement remained true but as time went by it became apparent that the scooter could be used with far more versatility and was an excellent all-round form of transport. That is why Innocenti developed the Lambretta, making it more powerful and a long-distance touring machine capable of carrying two people. The TV 175, with a top speed of over 60mph and long-range, was the epitome of this and was the ideal tourer.

It was in production before any motorways had been built in the UK, so it came as a shock when the Daily Mail newspaper reported that scooters should not be intended for use on the new motorway network. This was in reference to the first section of the M1 linking London to the Midlands. Though the report wasn't aimed directly at the Lambretta, it was quite obvious that it did apply to it. The report was printed by the paper in October 1959, just after that stretch of the motorway had been opened and it infuriated the scooter companies. None more so than Peter Agg, who was very angry at what he called absurd and unfounded allegations.

He vowed to prove the *Daily Mail* wrong and, in the process, prove how good the Lambretta was on these new stretches of fast open roads. Rather than use a TV 175, he made the challenge even more remarkable by taking a brand new Li 150 series two and having it travel up the entire length of the motorway in one go. The rider chosen to undertake the challenge was Brian Gibbs, with Peter Agg instructing him to take a spares order from the factory in Croydon to Chas E Cope & Sons – a Lambretta dealer based in Coventry. The journey took him along the entire 62-mile stretch of motorway that Daily Mail was referring to. Running at almost full throttle, he completed the motorway section in one hour and 15 minutes. The entire 140-mile journey took just over two and a half hours.

Having ensured that the media was aware of the trip beforehand, Gibbs was interviewed afterwards. He stated that not only did the Lambretta perform perfectly, but it was ideally suited to the new modern motorways of the UK. There is no doubt that Peter Agg was incensed by the initial report, but he had turned the situation around to concoct an easy marketing stunt, with Gibbs' trek being covered in many other newspapers. Regardless, he had proved the *Daily Mail* wrong. The newspaper failed to respond and the case was closed – with Lambretta having demonstrated that it definitely should not be banned from the motorway network.

Brian Gibbs pictured during his stint on the M1 motorway en route to Coventry to prove the *Daily Mail* wrong

5
The mystery of the Lambretta J range

Despite lower capacity Lambretta models being produced in each range, such as the Li 125, they still had the same chassis dimension and layout as the bigger models and cost a similar amount to produce. With many other manufacturers producing smaller lightweight machines, Piaggio having done so in 1963 with the Vespa 50, Innocenti needed to have something similar in its lineup. It had been developing a new range since the beginning of the decade, and this was now ready to go into production. The 100cc model was branded the Cento for obvious reasons, and the 125 version was the 'I' 125, with the 'I' standing for Innocenti. There would be a 50cc version also using the 'I' symbol, even though it seemed odd that they didn't have a specific name like the Cento.

That model reached the UK shores first, followed soon after by the 125, but it seems there was some confusion in the translation. The 'I' logo had a swept curve on the bottom, and, because it wasn't done in capital letters, there was a square above for the dot. Here is where the confusion started.

Innocenti sent over a load of advertising and technical literature to Lambretta Concessionaires to promote the new models and the man in charge of sorting it all was L. G. Clark, head of export sales. For a while, he sat there confused, reading through the paperwork and looking for the machine's name. He eventually came to the conclusion that the logo represented the letter 'J', even though there was no letter 'J' in the Italian alphabet, so Innocenti wouldn't have used it. Clark, having misread what was printed, without any thought, named the scooter J 125. All the other models in the range carried the same letter logo on their bodywork, so he called it the J range.

No one thought to question his line of reasoning, and so the name stayed with the scooter from that point on. In reality, there was now a Lambretta range with the wrong name. A good while later, the mistake was realised by Bob Wilkinson, who was working as head of the advertising department, but it was too late – the J range name had stuck – so it was left as it was. It was probably a good thing to do because changing

The J 125 Starstream being put through its paces during a UK road test

Innocenti literature showing the font used for the letter 'I'

In the UK, that was translated to the letter 'J'

Lambretta introduce J range

IN styling and construction the new J range of Lambrettas is based on the Cento introduced early in 1964. At present only the 125 c.c. model is available, but a 50 c.c. version should be in the dealers sometime in the Spring. Because, like the Cento, the frame in the J range is of monocoque assembly, it has been possible to trim manufacturing costs. The price of the J 125, for instance, is £139 18s. 9d., which, including the recently introduced 15 per cent surcharge, is only £2 more than the previous 125 model in the Lambretta range. The price of the J 50 has not yet been announced.

Brief specification of the J 125 :

Engine : Lambretta 122.48 c.c. single-cylinder blower cooled two-stroke ; bore 57mm. ; stroke 48mm. ; compression ratio 7.45 : 1 ; claimed b.h.p. 5.15 at 5,300 r.p.m.

Transmission : Three-speed gearbox, overall ratios 14.025, 8.437 and 5.663 : 1 ; primary drive by chain in oil bath ; gear final drive. Multiple disc clutch in oil bath.

Frame : Welded pressed steel.

Suspension : Trailing link front forks ; trailing arm engine-transmission unit with coil spring and hydraulic damper.

Wheels : Interchangeable, tyres 3.00 x 10in.

Brakes : 6in. diam. drum type.

Tank : Pressed steel, total capacity 1¼ gallons, reserve 1¾ pints.

Lubrication : Petroil mixture 50 : 1 ratio.

Electrical equipment : Flywheel generator ; ignition coil ; 25/25w. headlamp ; 5w. pilot light ; 3/15w. tail and stop light ; all bulbs 6v. ; horn ; handlebar lighting control unit.

General equipment : Speedometer, dualseat, centre stand, kit of tools.

Dimensions : Overall length 5ft. 6½in. ; overall height 3ft. 4¼in. ; saddle height from ground 2ft. 7½in. ; overall width 2ft. 8in.

Because of the improved power-to-weight ratio (monocoque construction is lighter than a comparable tubular frame) the manufacturers claim better performance (a cruising speed of 50 m.p.h. is quoted), and fuel consumption at 118 m.p.g.

Magazine reports also used the letter 'J' because Lambretta Concessionaires had instructed them

L. G. Clark
Purchasing &
Shipping Manager

Export Sales.
Accessory Administration & Development.
Accessory Newsletters.

L. G. Clark was the man responsible for mistakenly establishing the J range monicker

Lambretta

Newsletter

LAMBRETTA J 50

TECHNICAL DETAILS

Dimensions and weights

Wheelbase	-	1190 mm.	=	48"
Max. length	-	1660 mm.	=	65.25"
Max. width (handlebar)	-	630 mm.	=	24.8"
Max. height (handlebar)	-	1000 mm.	=	39.55"
Saddle height	-	760 mm.	=	39.55"
Seats	-	1		

Weight - Unladen - running order - 78 Kg. (171.6 lbs) Approx.

Performance

Max. Speed	-	56 K.m.p. (35 mph)
Consumption (to CUNA rules)		170 m.p.gall.

Engine Transmission Group

Single cylinder with counterposed current scavenging -

Capacity	-	49.8 cc
Bore	-	38 mm
Stroke	-	44 mm
Compression ratio	-	7.75
Max. effective power	-	1.5 HP
Max. revs at max power	-	4500 R.P.M. (to I.H. Code Rules)

The cylinder is in special cast iron, inclined towards the front 9°. Cylinder head in light alloy pressure cast. Piston cast in light alloy. Con rod in high resistance steel, with needle roller small end. Split crankshaft on ball bearings. Ignition by flywheel magneto with external H.T. Coil. Fixed advance ignition. Carburettor twist grip controlled. Cooling by forced cold air through flywheel fan.

Clutch	-	Multiple disc in oil bath.
Transmission	-	By chain with pinion sprocket ratio of 14/45 (1.3214)

Gear Box - On rear axle, 3 speed, twist grip combined with clutch and controlled by double cable. Gear indicator on twist grip boss.

Ratios at gear box -

1st	-	10/69	-	1 to 6.9
2nd	-	16/64	-	1 to 4.0
3rd	-	22/56	-	1 to 2.55

The technical press release sent out to UK dealers for the J 50, signalling its impending release in 1966

LAMBRETTA "50" *and* "125"

Best kept secret at the Show, the new 50 c.c. *Lambretta* appears on the stand without a price tag and the information that it will not be available at the earliest until next Spring.

The new "J" model is a clever development of the pressed steel chassis/body layout as used on the successful "Cento" model to take the proven 125 c.c. engine of the "Li". It also nearly manages to beat the new excess import duty and is most attractively priced of the range.

A news snip from a magazine also announcing the J 50 in the UK – but it never happened

the name now would seem like a rebranding exercise, and sales were struggling across the entire J range. The public might think it was to try and relaunch something that wasn't working rather than correcting a naming error. The other thinking is probably that the 'I' range wouldn't have the same appeal, so they left it as it was.

By 1966, there was another strange occurrence: despite being available for more than 18 months, the 50cc version hadn't been on sale in the UK. All that was about to change, however. Three demonstration models were sent over from Innocenti and put through their paces at the factory and by well-respected riders. This was shortly followed by a factory press release and specification sheet regarding its intended release, but strangely, it never happened. Sales of the Cento were rapidly declining, with many customers complaining it was rather flimsy and that its lack of power made it hard work in modern traffic and over long distances. With much better options available from the Slimstyle range, it made those in charge think that launching it might be a bad idea. Maurie Knight, now head of sales, openly admitted that he didn't like the J range due to the feedback he was getting from customers. The worry was that a model with even less power, and by a considerable margin, would simply fail in showrooms.

By now, the shift to the motorcar was taking precedence, with two-wheeled sales declining rapidly. The right models needed to be made available in order to maintain public appeal. Even though the J 50 had a competitive price, that wasn't enough to take the risk; therefore, it was decided not to stock it. The machine may have been ideal in small Italian villages, but it wasn't suited to the UK roads. As time would tell, when the Vega struggled years later, Lambretta Concessionaires had made the correct decision. Both the incorrect branding of the range, and the 50cc version that was thought to be available but never was, are two myths that were never questioned until recently but can now be settled.

6
The Police Lambretta

Police around the globe have commonly used motorcycles as a form of transport, and few more so than in the UK. Throughout the time of Lambretta production, the British motorcycle industry was regularly supplying two-wheelers to constabularies across the country. Supplying these machines wasn't as easy as it sounded though since there was stiff competition. Nevertheless, Lambretta Concessionaires was inspired to try selling Lambrettas to police forces because it could potentially result in a very lucrative contract and a significant volume of units being shifted.

The earliest attempts made were to try interesting police in the LD, but there was one main problem: the electrical system's power. The low-output 6-volt system would be required to power other items such as horns, flashing lights and a radio. That meant even less current would be left over for the main lights – and it was a given that the scooters would be operated at night. A dim headlight would make the scooter effectively unusable for police work.

A demonstration machine was sent out for evaluation and rejected for this very reason, so a special 12-volt upgrade was carried out at the factory. The improvement in visibility was tremendous but still not quite enough to convince those who made the decisions to place an order. The upgraded LD was returned, whereupon Peter Agg sold it to his cousin, making him the only person with a factory 12-volt Lambretta – much to the envy of his friends.

Attempts to try and sell later models proved more successful, with some series two models being supplied. The real breakthrough was the series three Slimstyle machine, which allowed for a much more refined design. With its great handling qualities and better performance, it was ideally suited for local

SPECIFICATION OF MACHINE FOR POLICE APPLICATION

LAMBRETTA 150 LI THIRD SERIES

FITTED EXTRAS OF LUCAS MANUFACTURE

Direction indicators	Model L 628 Pt. No. 54057078
	Main Bulbs 6V 18W S.C.C.
	Warning light 6V 0.6W
	Flasher Unit Model F L 5 6V 36W
	Operating Switch Model 94 SA
Inspection light	Model 100 Pt. No. 54057132
	Bulb 6V 24W
	Switch P S 7
Flashing light Model	
	Main Bulb 6V 18 W
	Operating Switch 65 S A
	Flasher unit F L 5 6V 18W
(Lambretta part)	Protection rubber 00670303
(Lambretta part)	Securing clip 20055060
Windtone Horns 6V	Model 9H Pt. No. 540.680.55
	Low note horn 540.680.16
	High note horn 540.680.17
	Relay Model GRA Pt. No. 33219

EXAMPLE OF APPLICATION

SWITCH POSITION :	POWER TAKEN :
Off - Radio receiving only	2 amps.
Pilot position - Radio plus pilot lights	3.5 amps.
Head position - Radio plus main lighting	6.9 amps.
With all equipment operating, balancing road speed	29/30 m.p.h.

SPECIAL POLICE ACCESSORIES

Inspection Light	Model 100 6v			
	Pt. No. 54057132	£ 2.	1.	3d.
Switch extra	Pt. No. P S 7	£ -.	8.	3d.
Windtone Horns	Model 9 H			
	Pt. No. 540.680.55	£ 4.	7.	9d. set.
Flashing Indicators	Model 628			
	Pt. No. 540.570.78	£ 4.	15.	0d. set.
Flashing Light (Blue)	Model			
	Pt. No. 65 S A			
	Flasher Unit	£ -.	13.	9d.
	Switch	£ -.	6.	6d.
Specially adapted Satellite Windscreen		£ 6.	6.	0d.

SUBJECT TO 33⅓% DISCOUNT

ACCESSORY FITTING CHARGES

Direction Indicators	£ 3.	10.	0d.
Inspection Light	£ -.	17.	6d.
Flashing Blue Light	£ 2.	0.	0d.
Windtone Horns	£ 1.	10.	0d.

The above charges include stripping down, rewiring and making good.

The list of extra equipment was impressive but required an upgraded electrical system to power it all

Lambretta Concessionaires launched the police Lambretta in 1964, attempting to sell it to constabularies across the country

constabularies. 12-volt electrics were fitted as standard, and the six-pole stator provided enough power to run a whole host of essential equipment and extras. Strangely, though, the model offered was a Li 150, when it would be expected that the TV 175 or TV 200 would have been better, with much more powerful engines.

The main reason the Li 150 was chosen was because, with all the extra equipment fitted, it was possible to make the machine slightly unbalanced. This had become noticeable with faster motorbikes, with riders even being blamed for certain accidents where they fell off at high speed. The Li 150 was guaranteed safe at 30mph with all the extra equipment, and around town on patrol that was all that was required, remembering many police either used a bicycle or got around by foot. Because the Li 150 was cheaper to buy than the TV models, it was more attractive to constabularies with a limited budget. However, some police forces did purchase the TV 200 in limited quantities because of its more powerful engine, and it was ideal for rural counties where greater distance travelling was required. Even so, the Li 150 remained the popular choice, and it is believed that several hundred were sold to different constabularies in the UK.

Though the Li 150 was the most common Police Lambretta, the series two Li 150 and TV 200 were also among the models used

7
The fake Li 150 Special

Innocenti unveiled the Li 150 special in 1963. It was, in theory, a sports version of the Li 150 series three and utilised the styling of the TV 200 with the heptagonal headlamp, wider horn casting grille and squared-off mudguard. It also had what at the time was regarded as the GT-style side panels with knuckleduster embellishers, giving the upgraded Li 150 a refreshing look. The engine had the same treatment with slightly more power and the advantage of a much closer ratio gearbox, improved acceleration, and a genuine top speed of 60mph.

It was a clever move by Innocenti because they had created a new model without a considerable budget being required to develop it. The bodywork would be painted in one colour, silver, which included the forks, hubs and wheels, and would be known as the Silver Special, even being badged as such towards the end of production in 1966. An all-gold version was also offered late on, as they attempted to sell them off. The Li 150 Special became an instant hit, selling well from day one with those wanting better performance but at less cost than the TV models.

The only colour image ever used for advertising featured the blue side panels. The gold Pacemaker logo was on the panel but didn't show up well in the photograph

The Li 150 Special was heavily advertised and always promoted as the Pacemaker in the UK

It was widely anticipated that it would do well in the UK and made it over in early 1964 to a huge fanfare. Before its launch, Peter Agg decided to rebrand it just as he had done the previous year with the TV 200, calling that the GT 200. This time, it would be the Li 150 Special Pacemaker, and there were stark references to the band Gerry and the Pacemakers, who had been hugely popular in 1963. The connection was cemented even further by the band's film Ferry Across the Mersey, which was recorded and released in 1964 and featured the band on Lambrettas, including a Pacemaker.

To make the monotone colour stand out, the side panels were offered in blue and did have the 'Pacemaker' script applied to the side of the panel using a gold foil sticker. Peter Agg wasted no time in launching a vast marketing campaign in the national press to promote it. Bob Wilkinson recalls the press shoot where Peter Insisted it be done immediately, but the problem was they didn't have a machine to hand.

The famous press image using a TV 200. With the front dampers removed. It was meant to look like a drum brake set-up, but it is possible to see the vent at the front for the disc. The white and two-tone colour scheme on the side panels was only ever used on the TV 200, another giveaway sign. The pacemaker emblem on the leg shields was never used on a production machine

A side view shot from the same photo session shows the disc brake and why customers complained when the production model of the Pacemaker didn't have one fitted

Agg being notorious for venting his anger if there was any delay, there was no option other than to use another model instead. A TV 200 was chosen, but the problem was they were only available in white with a narrower colour flash on the panel, which was different from it being painted all one colour. The other noticeable difference was the TV 200 had a disc brake fitted, whereas the Pacemaker still used the drum brake.

For the photoshoot, they used male and female models from a local agency, and the now-famous image used the female model with the machine from a side angle. To try and hide the differences, the front dampers were removed; again, the Pacemaker didn't have them fitted, but it was just possible to make out the front disc brake to those with a keen eye. This didn't hide the fact that the paint scheme was different, but it was the best they could do at short notice without having the correct machine to photograph. A side-on image taken showing the disc brake in its entirety was a bit of a problem since this completely gave the game away.

Bob remembers customers enquiring why there was no disc brake fitted to the Pacemaker, and awkward conversations ensued on more than one occasion. Also, the colour scheme was different, and the Pacemaker script on the leg shields was only used in the photoshoot again, leaving customers slightly confused. In today's world of trading standards, such a stunt would not be allowed, but things were far more relaxed back then. Regardless, the images released to the press were of a fake Pacemaker that never officially existed.

8
The Lambretta hovercraft

For years, various rumours circulated about the Lambretta hovercraft, where it was made, by whom, and whether it went into production. The answer to the final part is no, because it was a private development created as a one-off. The confusion comes about because the name 'Lambrettair' is displayed down the side of it using the traditional Lambretta font, so it was presumed the company made it. It was, in fact, the creation of Anthony Tessier, who was on a course at Shoreditch College in 1968 and, as part of his thesis, had to create a working hovercraft.

Tony had been heavily involved with Lambretta Concessionaires, being part of their team that had competed in the Milan-Taranto and Moto Giro races in Italy. He worked briefly at the Croydon-based factory in 1966 before moving to Supertune. Having worked closely with Bob Wilkinson, who was now the chief advertising and PR manager at Lambretta Concessionaires, he explained that not one but two Lambretta engines would power the hovercraft he was building. Keen to get in on the act and realising there was huge publicity potential to be had from it, Bob offered to supply the engines for it directly from the factory.

That is when they came up with the Lambrettair name, a take on the word Lambretta, displayed on both sides of the machine down the length of its skirt. Once Tony knew he had the backing of the factory, he got on with building the hovercraft. He needed two engines, one to create the lift and the other for the drive, but he would modify them as they didn't need to run through the gearbox transmission but instead directly from the cush drive. Other Lambretta parts used, such as the petrol tank, came from a J range model. Once it was built to pass the exam, Tony was required to carry two people in it down a course which was the length of a football pitch, on the recreation ground near the college.

The examiners didn't give it a chance and Tony angrily told them to place six people on board and, once they were strapped in, gave it full throttle, achieving the distance required with ease. Using shortened silencers, the noise was ear-shattering, not to mention the dust created by the giant fans. Both Lambretta engines performed flawlessly, much to the disbelief of the examiners, but Tony had known all along that they would create the power required. So happy was Bob that the PR stunts continued, and this being 1969, he did it to the maximum potential. Photoshoots were carried out with the controller wearing a space suit as it was

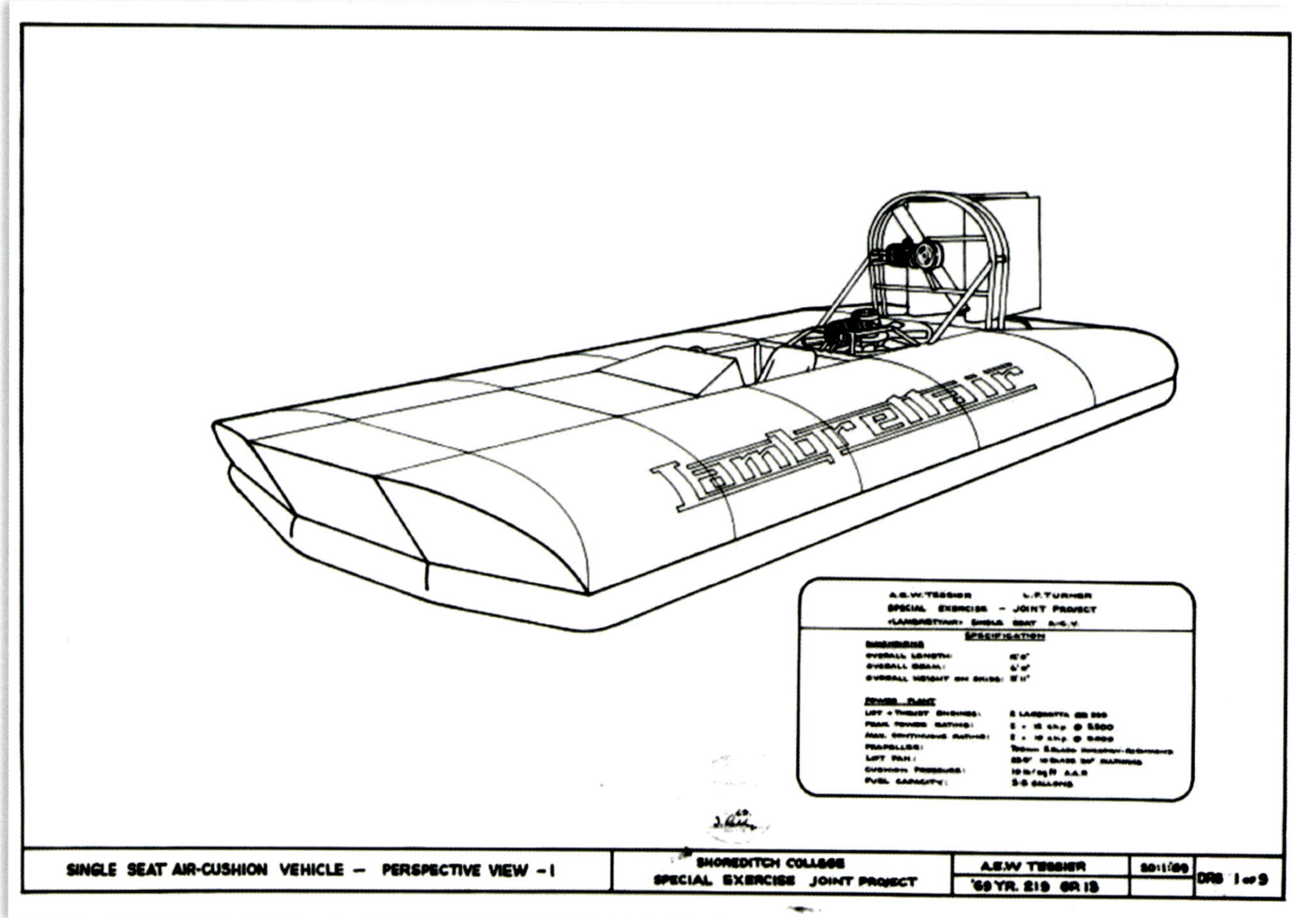

One of the original drawings made by Tony for the hovercraft, which had the Lambrettair logo down the side

Lambretta

Lambretta Concessionaires Ltd
Lambretta House Purley Way Croydon
CR9 4HD England Phone: 01 686 2499
Telex: 21138 Cables: Lambretta Croydon

SCOOTER POWERED HOVERCRAFT TO MAKE TRIAL

TAKE OFF AT BRANDS HATCH ON APRIL 3

Press Preview for International Motor Cycle Show

A scooter without wheels which rides on air over land or water is to make its debut at Brands Hatch circuit on Thursday, April 3, at the Press preview for the International Cycle and Motor Cycle Show, opening at the Hotel Metropole, Brighton on April 5.

Known as the "Lambrettair," it is powered by two 200 c.c. Lambretta engines - the same engines which power the new Lambretta Grand Prix scooter which is also being shown for the first time at the preview.

It is being built by 25-year old Tony Tessier of Greenford, Middlesex and 21-year old Laurie Turner of Leek, Staffs, both of whom are student handicraft teachers at the Shoreditch College of Education, near Windsor.

Tony got the idea three years ago after preparing a thesis on light hovercraft and he and Laurie started designing "Lambrettair" in September 1967. They spent 12 months on the drawing board, during which time the craft they were planning to build was also the subject of a symposium at the Hoverclub of Great Britain.

As both these students are on a three-year course in advanced metal-work, they decided to construct their hovercraft in metal - most home-made ones are of wood - but made sure, first of all, of obtaining the advice and re-assurance of a metallurgist from the British Hovercraft Corporation.

They started building in February this year and have spent 500 man hours on the job. Their craft is made of 250-ft of 20-guage steel tubing and 34-sq. yrds. of 26-guage aluminium and is 12-ft long, 6-ft. wide and 1-ft. 3-in. high. It weighs 420-lbs.

The press release made by Bob Wilkinson which mentioned the vehicle being powered by a pair of Grand Prix 200 engines when, in fact, they were from a TV 200

Getting ready to start the hovercraft up. Note the J range petrol tank sitting on top of the fan and the chequered flags on the fins, which were the same ones used on the front leg shields of the Grand Prix 150

Peter Davis of the LCGB is at the controls, with Lambretta racer Bev Flannigan as a passenger.

Once fired up the huge fan underneath would kick out vast plumes of dust

just before the moon landings were about to happen, and the space race gripped the world.

A huge press launch was carried out, and the release notes mentioned that the hovercraft was powered by two brand new Grand Prix 200 engines, which had just entered production in March, to make it sound even more exciting. Tony revealed years later that the statement wasn't entirely accurate and that they were not Grand Prix 200 engines. They were a pair of unused TV 200 engines which were perfectly good enough, and at the time, no one noticed otherwise.

Once Tony had completed the coursework, he moved on to new pastures, and the hovercraft remained there, used as a demonstration piece for students. The only remaining mystery is what happened to it because, despite Tony's best efforts, he still can't trace its whereabouts, but it's possible it could still be somewhere out there.

9
Who introduced the Lambretta to the UK?

It has always been presumed that Lambretta Concessionaires was the company that made Lambretta what it is in the UK, which is true. It is also assumed that it was James and Peter Agg who started it all up, but that is where the truth has become somewhat distorted because it wasn't them at all. The Lambretta began to establish itself in Italy with the Model A and its successors, Models B and C, would propel it forward. As the 1940s ended, it was no surprise that Innocenti wanted to export the Lambretta to other countries.

It was an unknown quantity outside of Italy, but news of it had reached the UK and a company called the British-Italian Trading Co had subsequently imported a small batch of Model B machines. Coverage was sporadic, besides the odd piece in a few motorcycle publications, which did little to help sales. Around the same time, a group of speedway riders were on international duty in Italy along with their mechanics, two of whom were Les Ashton and Donato Royale. Both men had motorcycle dealerships in Wimbledon and Aldershot, and they couldn't help but notice these small two-stroke machines buzzing around the capital. Les was the more curious and, without hesitation, made enquiries and soon found out it was the Lambretta.

He was an entrepreneurial character and realised they might be worth a punt back in the UK. Innocenti was more than happy to take an enquiry and explained that a company in the UK had already imported some but that there was no concession set up yet. Once back home, the men approached the British-Italian Trading Co. and offered to take their remaining stock of Model B machines, and with the company struggling to sell them, a deal was struck. Offering the

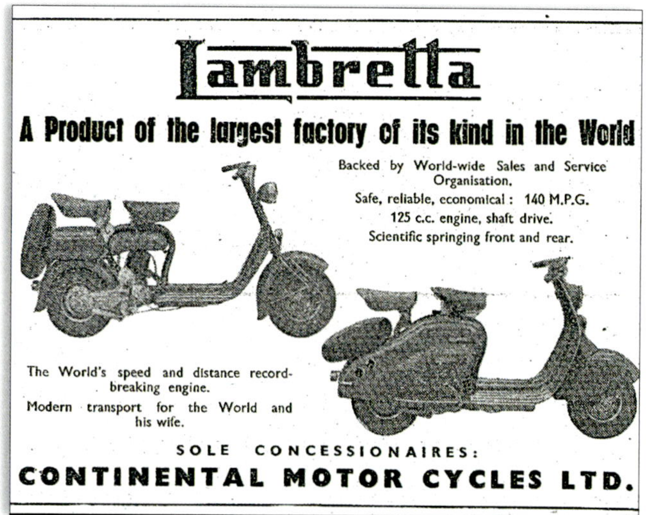

The first Lambretta advert in the UK listed Continental Motorcycles as the sole concession

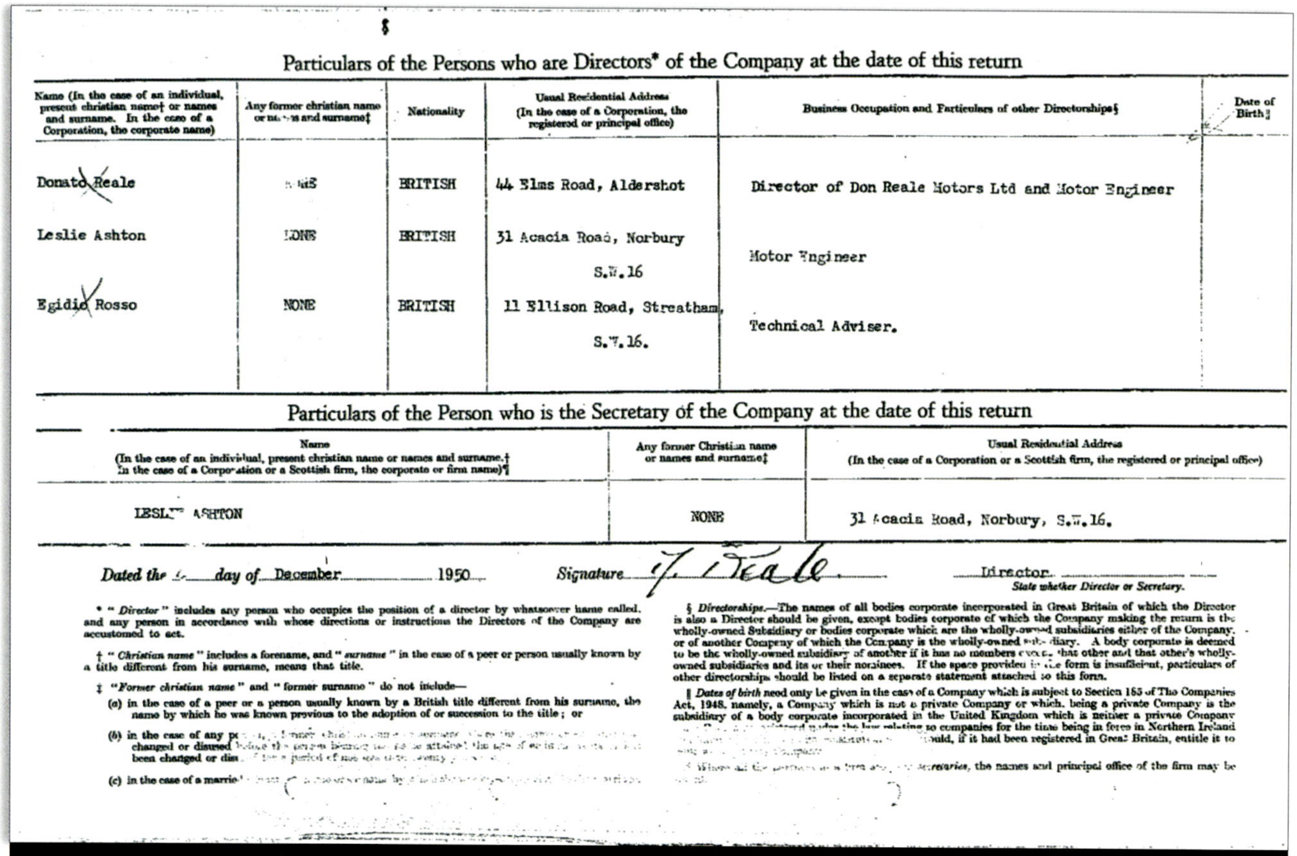

Particulars of the Persons who are Directors* of the Company at the date of this return

Name (In the case of an individual, present christian name† or names and surname. In the case of a Corporation, the corporate name)	Any former christian name or names and surname‡	Nationality	Usual Residential Address (In the case of a Corporation, the registered or principal office)	Business Occupation and Particulars of other Directorships§	Date of Birth‖
Donato Reale	[illegible]	BRITISH	44 Elms Road, Aldershot	Director of Don Reale Motors Ltd and Motor Engineer	
Leslie Ashton	NONE	BRITISH	31 Acacia Road, Norbury S.W.16	Motor Engineer	
Egidio Rosso	NONE	BRITISH	11 Ellison Road, Streatham, S.W.16.	Technical Adviser.	

Particulars of the Person who is the Secretary of the Company at the date of this return

Name (In the case of an individual, present christian name or names and surname.† In the case of a Corporation or a Scottish firm, the corporate or firm name)¶	Any former Christian name or names and surname‡	Usual Residential Address (In the case of a Corporation or a Scottish firm, the registered or principal office)
LESLIE ASHTON	NONE	31 Acacia Road, Norbury, S.W.16.

Dated the … day of December 1950 Signature [signature] Director
State whether Director or Secretary.

* "Director" includes any person who occupies the position of a director by whatsoever name called, and any person in accordance with whose directions or instructions the Directors of the Company are accustomed to act.

† "Christian name" includes a forename, and "surname" in the case of a peer or person usually known by a title different from his surname, means that title.

‡ "Former christian name" and "former surname" do not include—
(a) in the case of a peer or a person usually known by a British title different from his surname, the name by which he was known previous to the adoption of or succession to the title; or
(b) in the case of any … changed or disused … been changed or dis…
(c) in the case of a marrie…

§ Directorships.—The names of all bodies corporate incorporated in Great Britain of which the Director is also a Director should be given, except bodies corporate of which the Company making the return is the wholly-owned Subsidiary or bodies corporate which are the wholly-owned subsidiaries either of the Company, or of another Company of which the Company is the wholly-owned subsidiary. A body corporate is deemed to be the wholly-owned subsidiary of another if it has no members except that other and that other's wholly-owned subsidiaries and its or their nominees. If the space provided in the form is insufficient, particulars of other directorships should be listed on a separate statement attached to this form.

‖ Dates of birth need only be given in the case of a Company which is subject to Section 185 of The Companies Act, 1948, namely, a Company which is not a private Company or which, being a private Company is the subsidiary of a body corporate incorporated in the United Kingdom which is neither a private Company … to companies for the time being in force in Northern Ireland … would, if it had been registered in Great Britain, entitle it to …

¶ … secretaries, the names and principal office of the firm may be …

The three listed directors, including Les and Don, as the first company to hold the Lambretta concession into the UK

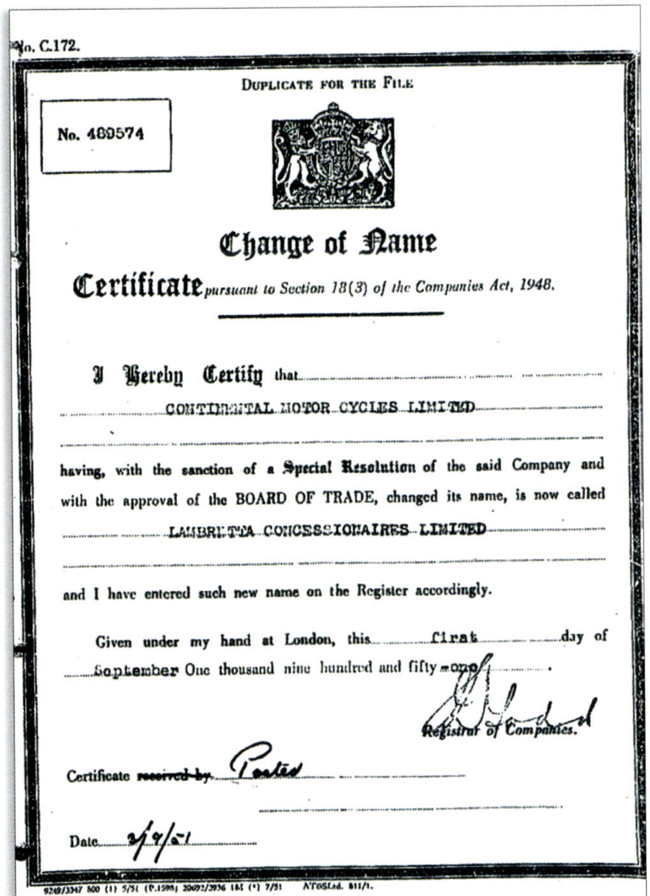

No. C.172.

DUPLICATE FOR THE FILE

No. 489574

Change of Name Certificate

pursuant to Section 18(3) of the Companies Act, 1948.

I Hereby Certify that CONTINENTAL MOTOR CYCLES LIMITED

having, with the sanction of a Special Resolution of the said Company and with the approval of the BOARD OF TRADE, changed its name, is now called LAMBRETTA CONCESSIONAIRES LIMITED

and I have entered such new name on the Register accordingly.

Given under my hand at London, this first day of September One thousand nine hundred and fifty-one.

Registrar of Companies.

Certificate ~~received by~~ Posted

Date 3/9/51

Nine months after Continental Motorcycles had been formed, the Aggs were now involved and the company name was changed to Lambretta Concessionaires

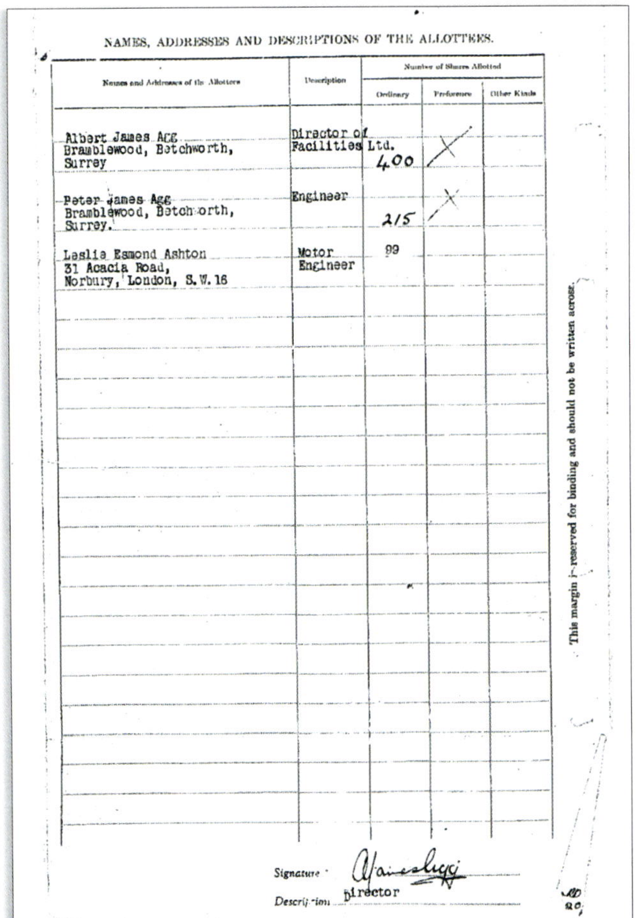

NAMES, ADDRESSES AND DESCRIPTIONS OF THE ALLOTTEES.

Names and Addresses of the Allottees	Description	Number of Shares Allotted: Ordinary	Preference	Other Kinds
Albert James Agg, Bramblewood, Betchworth, Surrey	Director of Facilities Ltd.	400	X	
Peter James Agg, Bramblewood, Betchworth, Surrey.	Engineer	215	X	
Leslie Esmond Ashton, 31 Acacia Road, Norbury, London, S.W.16	Motor Engineer	99		

This margin is reserved for binding and should not be written across.

Signature

Description Director

The new share listing, which showed the Aggs had the majority holding of the company

scooters through shops dedicated to motorcycles was a much better option. Before long, they sold most of the stock and, realising they might be on to something good, approached Innocenti about becoming the sole concession in the UK. This was agreed, so in December 1950, they formed Continental Motorcycles Limited along with a third man, dedicated purely to importing the Lambretta into the UK.

By this time, Innocenti was producing new models, the C and LC, which would be the first Lambretta models the newly created Continental Motorcycles would sell. Even though they knew the industry well

Les Ashton's business, Rapid Motors, was the ideal platform to start trading the Lambretta

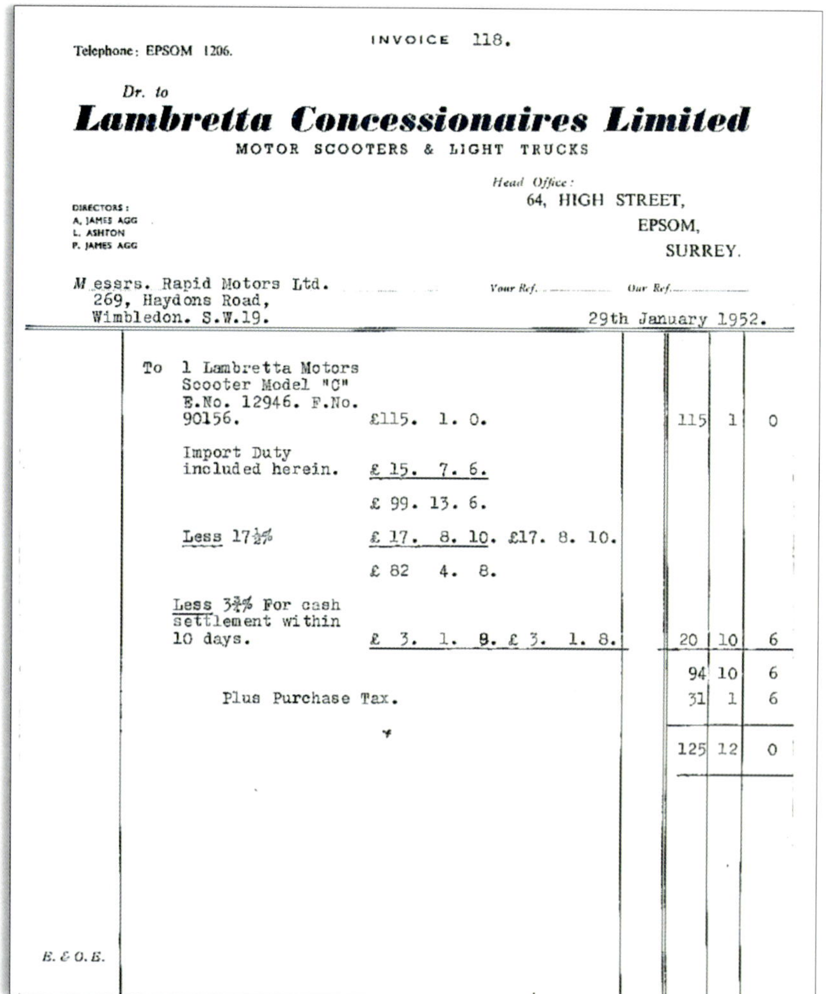

Telephone: EPSOM 1206.

INVOICE 118.

Dr. to

Lambretta Concessionaires Limited

MOTOR SCOOTERS & LIGHT TRUCKS

Head Office:
64, HIGH STREET,
EPSOM,
SURREY.

DIRECTORS:
A. JAMES AGG
L. ASHTON
P. JAMES AGG

Messrs. Rapid Motors Ltd.
269, Haydons Road,
Wimbledon. S.W.19.

Your Ref. .... Our Ref. ....

29th January 1952.

			£	s.	d.
To 1 Lambretta Motors Scooter Model "C" E.No. 12946. F.No. 90156.	£115. 1. 0.		115	1	0
Import Duty included herein.	£ 15. 7. 6.				
	£ 99. 13. 6.				
Less 17½%	£ 17. 8. 10.	£17. 8. 10.			
	£ 82 4. 8.				
Less 3¾% For cash settlement within 10 days.	£ 3. 1. 8.	£ 3. 1. 8.	20	10	6
			94	10	6
Plus Purchase Tax.			31	1	6
			125	12	0

E. & O. E.

One of the last invoices from January 1952 for the sale of a Lambretta where Les Ashton was listed as a director of the company

A few years later, Les still traded as Rapid Motors, having just secured the concession for the French Terrot scooter, placed an ad in the motorcycle press. In it, he mentioned that this was the company that introduced the Lambretta to England

Les Ashton, who was responsible for starting the Lambretta success story in the UK

and with their shops being the ideal platform to trade them, it took a few months for Les and Don to grow the company. Sure enough, they did, but the problem was sticking to the agreement with Innocenti; they had to order a more significant number of machines, and because they had to pay up front, they struggled with cashflow. Don Royale had an idea to bring in a third party, not to run the business but to give it a cash injection as a silent partner. Les wasn't happy about the situation but agreed with there being no other option apparent, even though Don had kept something from him.

The people he introduced were a father and son, James and Peter Agg, who were pretty affluent but with little interest in anything like the Lambretta. Don's financial problems went much deeper than the cashflow he needed for Continental Motorcycles Ltd because the Aggs had already lent him money regarding his other business affairs. Before long, and further in debt to them, he repaid some of it back by selling his shares in Continental with the Aggs also acquiring those of the company's third owner.

This meant the Aggs and Les Ashton now owned it, but worryingly for him, they now had the majority shareholding. This meant they could control decisions, the first of which was to change the company's name to Lambretta Concessionaires Limited, which made sense as the importation of the Lambretta was its sole purpose. Les agreed to this, but friction between him and Peter worsened.

The company was starting to have some success, and though Peter Agg wasn't that bothered about the Lambretta, the businessman in him made him realise they were onto something big. His idea was to take the Lambretta nationwide as quickly as possible, but Les and he began disagreeing on how to proceed. Before long, it became a caustic environment, and working together was untenable.

Sadly for Les, he was in the minority with his smaller shareholding and, therefore, was forced out by the Aggs. The split was somewhat acrimonious and made even worse for Les as within a year of him leaving the company was surging ahead due to the popularity of the Lambretta.

Years later, and still in the trade, Les would often claim that he had bought the Lambretta over to the UK first and, therefore, was responsible for its success. Technically, that wasn't true because the British-Italian Trading Co had done so just before him, but he had set up the concession, which was where the story really began. The falling out between him and Peter Agg was so bad that Peter refused to acknowledge Les regarding the success of Lambretta Concessionaires or his involvement right up until he died. The undeniable truth is that Les Ashton started the Lambretta story in the UK and should be forever remembered for doing so.

10
Was the Lambretta advertised on television?

Throughout the 1950s, Lambretta advertising in the UK progressively gained more comprehensive coverage as Lambretta Concessionaires attempted to corner the two-wheeled market. Doing so required a huge budget, as advertising in the right places wasn't cheap. With sales rising year on year, it was agreed that a certain percentage of the profits should be spent this way and the amount rose accordingly depending on how sales went. Coverage in major cities was extensive, from the sides of buses to train stations, basically putting the scooter in

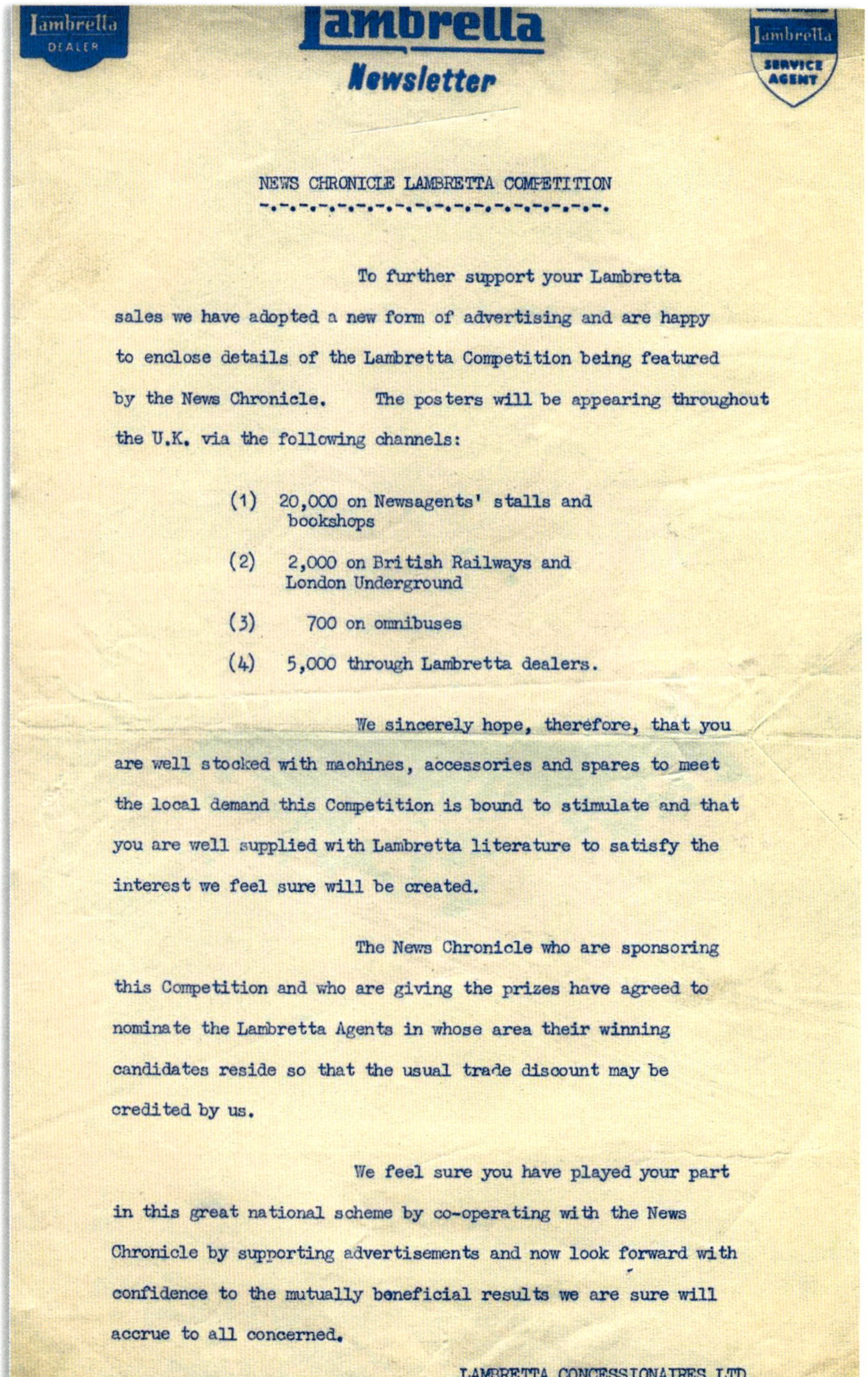
Lambretta DEALER

Lambretta

Newsletter

Lambretta SERVICE AGENT

NEWS CHRONICLE LAMBRETTA COMPETITION

To further support your Lambretta sales we have adopted a new form of advertising and are happy to enclose details of the Lambretta Competition being featured by the News Chronicle. The posters will be appearing throughout the U.K. via the following channels:

(1) 20,000 on Newsagents' stalls and bookshops

(2) 2,000 on British Railways and London Underground

(3) 700 on omnibuses

(4) 5,000 through Lambretta dealers.

We sincerely hope, therefore, that you are well stocked with machines, accessories and spares to meet the local demand this Competition is bound to stimulate and that you are well supplied with Lambretta literature to satisfy the interest we feel sure will be created.

The News Chronicle who are sponsoring this Competition and who are giving the prizes have agreed to nominate the Lambretta Agents in whose area their winning candidates reside so that the usual trade discount may be credited by us.

We feel sure you have played your part in this great national scheme by co-operating with the News Chronicle by supporting advertisements and now look forward with confidence to the mutually beneficial results we are sure will accrue to all concerned.

LAMBRETTA CONCESSIONAIRES LTD.

The level of advertising the Lambretta in the UK started to reach an immense scale by the mid-1950s, but there was still one area that it didn't cover: television

Lambretta

Lambretta Concessionaires Limited.

HEAD OFFICE & SALES ● 424/426 KINGSTON ROAD, RAYNES PARK S.W.20 ● Tel. CHErrywood 2204 (5 lines)
SERVICE STATION ● 213/219 THE BROADWAY, WIMBLEDON S.W.19 ● Tel. LIBerty 7621 (3 lines)
STORES & ACCESSORIES ● 221/227 THE BROADWAY, WIMBLEDON S.W.19 ● Tel. CHErrywood 2232 (2 lines)

A D V E R T I S I N G

You cannot fail to have noticed that one of our competitors has suddenly launched out on a national advertising scheme of some considerable scale, making much of the fact that their Italian parent company have sold from production over 1,000,000 throughout the world, as opposed to our own consistent but nevertheless considerable national scheme with which we have supported you throughout the season to help you assist Lambretta in establishing the highest scooter sales, not only in the world (where the million mark was passed many months ago) but, what is more important to you - the British dealer - the highest scooter sales in the United Kingdom.

However, never let it be said that Aggs of Lambretta will let the gauntlet fall unchallenged and, therefore, upon request to our representatives you will receive full details of a most extensive advertising scheme in your support, not disturbing the consistent press advertising with which we have supported you throughout 1956, in a completely new media - I.T.V. No less than sixty "showings" have been booked for the period 22nd July to 26th August - your peak selling period - giving direct Lambretta support to your efforts via this medium which is showing such good results throughout the country.

Please ask your area Lambretta representative for details of this scheme which has been timed to improve your sales at the peak selling period.

LAMBRETTA CONCESSIONAIRES LIMITED.

16th July, 1956.

After seeing advertising ramping up for the Vespa, the biggest rival to the Lambretta, Peter Agg went a step further by announcing a television campaign in 1956

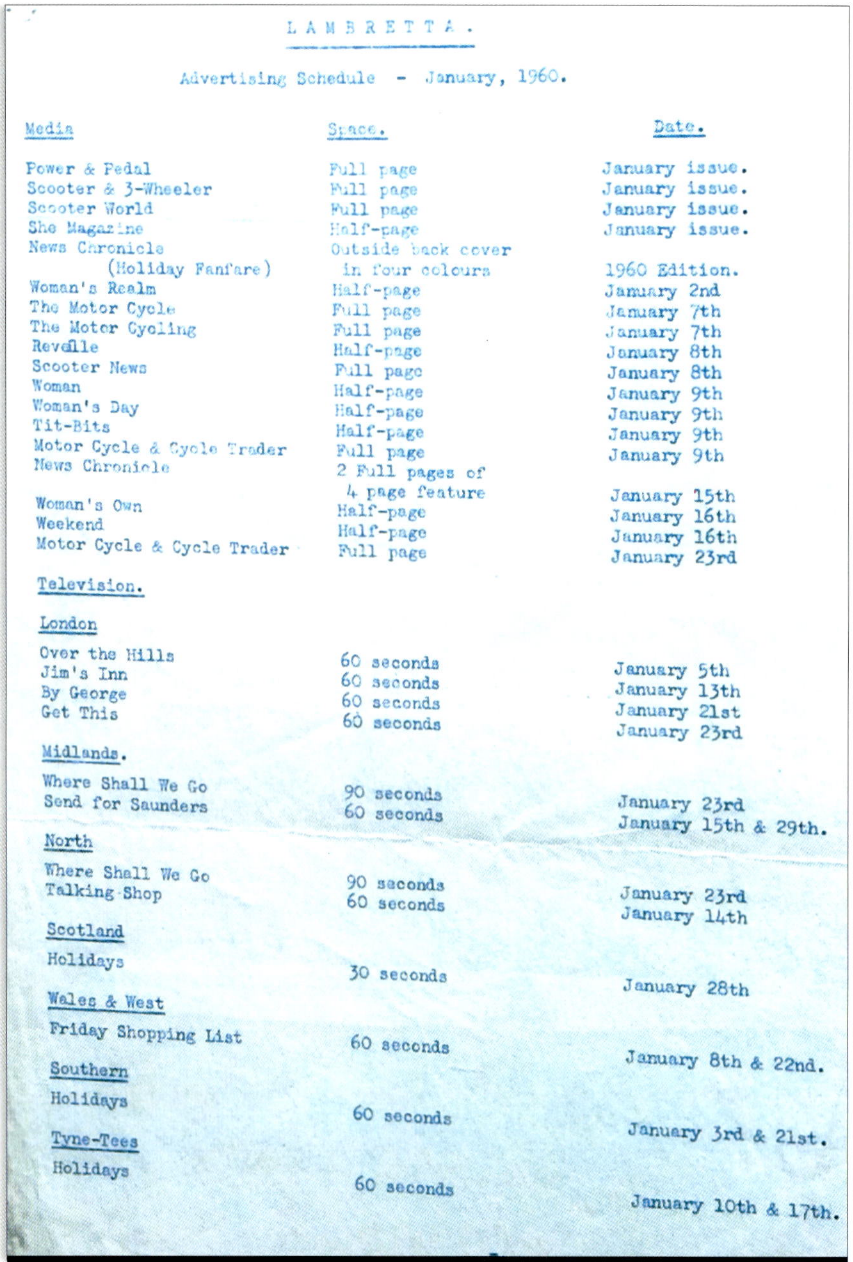

LAMBRETTA.

Advertising Schedule - January, 1960.

Media	Space.	Date.
Power & Pedal	Full page	January issue.
Scooter & 3-Wheeler	Full page	January issue.
Scooter World	Full page	January issue.
She Magazine	Half-page	January issue.
News Chronicle (Holiday Fanfare)	Outside back cover in four colours	1960 Edition.
Woman's Realm	Half-page	January 2nd
The Motor Cycle	Full page	January 7th
The Motor Cycling	Full page	January 7th
Reveille	Half-page	January 8th
Scooter News	Full page	January 8th
Woman	Half-page	January 9th
Woman's Day	Half-page	January 9th
Tit-Bits	Half-page	January 9th
Motor Cycle & Cycle Trader	Full page	January 9th
News Chronicle	2 Full pages of 4 page feature	
Woman's Own	Half-page	January 15th
Weekend	Half-page	January 16th
Motor Cycle & Cycle Trader	Full page	January 16th
		January 23rd
Television.		
London		
Over the Hills	60 seconds	January 5th
Jim's Inn	60 seconds	January 13th
By George	60 seconds	January 21st
Get This	60 seconds	January 23rd
Midlands.		
Where Shall We Go	90 seconds	January 23rd
Send for Saunders	60 seconds	January 15th & 29th.
North		
Where Shall We Go	90 seconds	January 23rd
Talking Shop	60 seconds	January 14th
Scotland		
Holidays	30 seconds	January 28th
Wales & West		
Friday Shopping List	60 seconds	January 8th & 22nd.
Southern		
Holidays	60 seconds	January 3rd & 21st.
Tyne-Tees		
Holidays	60 seconds	January 10th & 17th.

That last known television advertising schedule for the Lambretta was carried out in January 1960 on no fewer than seven of the ITV franchises across the nation

front of anyone using public transport. Nationally, it was advertised in magazines and newspapers with the idea that a person reading a newspaper in the morning, then going to work and then eventually returning home would be exposed to the Lambretta brand every step of the way.

There was, however, a sizeable gap in this round-the-clock approach: the evening time. Once sitting at home and relaxing after tea, potential customers would switch off from their daily lives, forgetting about it. What if they could still be exposed to the Lambretta through the power of television? By the mid to late 1950s, most households owned one, and the evening was when it was viewed the most. While the BBC didn't allow advertising, the independent channel (ITV), which began in 1955, did. Still in its infancy, broadcasts were nevertheless paid for, at least in part, by companies advertising on it. ITV had a host of regional network franchises, which began to build up, and this meant increased exposure potential for any advertisers.

Seeing this opportunity, Lambretta Concessionaires embarked on an ambitious plan to advertise the Lambretta across the independent network. During the summer months of 1956, a series of more than 60 adverts for the LD model were broadcast between programmes in the evening slot. This now meant that the customer would be exposed to the Lambretta from the moment they got up until they went to sleep at night.

The process also created a new slogan: "The Lambretta… as seen on TV". It was something no other manufacturer at the time could claim. There is evidence that this practice was continued until the beginning of the 1960s, when the advertising budget was slowly being cut back, meaning this would be the end of Lambretta advertising on UK television. Despite proof of it happening, no adverts seem to have survived. However, in today's world of social media, it can't be ruled out that somewhere in the future a clip may resurface.

11
Was the Lambretta designed to run on a 4% or 2% oil mixture?

For many years there has been significant debate among Lambretta owners as to what the correct oil mixture to run in the engine is. While that debate still rages, even when the scooter was still in production information on the correct percentage to use could sometimes be confusing. The handbook, running-in instructions on the leg shields, and service books all said to use a 4% mixture and that this must always be adhered to. The crude method of adding the oil to the fuel could be easy to forget, and measuring it wasn't easy either. The best way was to use a measuring jug, working out the percentage by the scale on the side, or use a two-stroke oil dispenser available at most petrol stations.

Just over a decade after the introduction of the Lambretta to the UK, Lambretta Concessionaires decided to change that ratio, lowering it to 2%. The benefit of this was twofold: less oil was being used, reducing the cost of running the machine, and more extended usage before the exhaust port coked up. That meant longer times between servicing, again making it cheaper for the owner. This resulted in another sales and advertising ploy because other manufacturers couldn't make the same claim.

BP also favoured the Lambretta and produced an oil branded BP-Zoom, which was designed to reduce carbon deposits in the engine

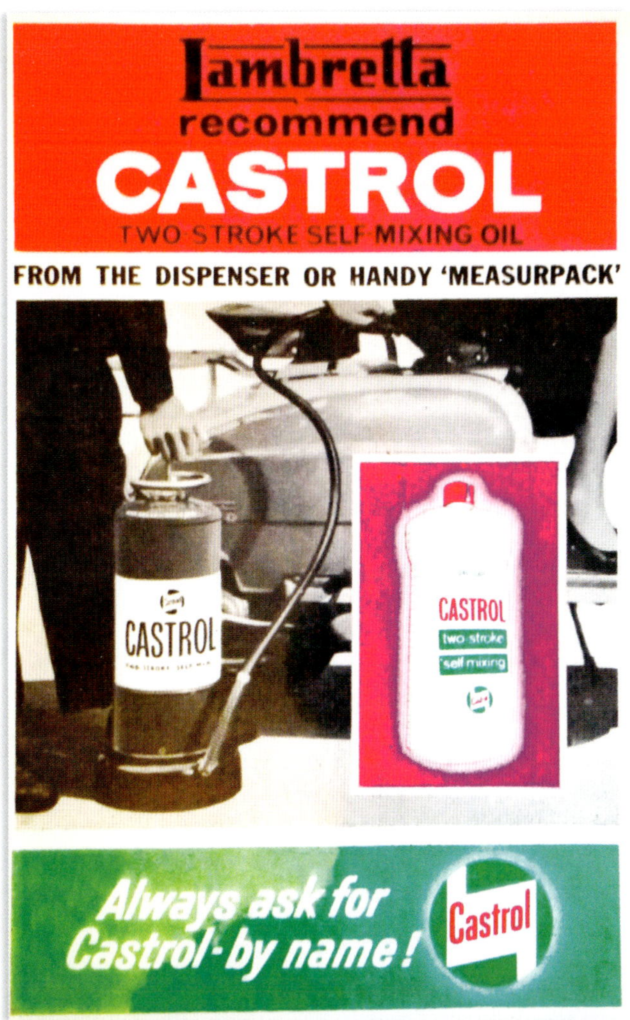

Castrol was keen to be associated with the Lambretta brand, and its two-stroke dispensing machines were commonplace at garages

Other companies such as Filtrate, were happy to sell the Lambretta owner a bottle of oil and measure it themselves

There were many recommended oil dealers but in the end, it still had to be manually mixed into the fuel tank

An incorrect mixture or cheap brand oil would always result in high carbon deposits, not only blocking the exhaust port but also the expansion box on a Lambretta, so reducing the mixture percentage would help

But the question remained, why do it now when it could have been done earlier? The answer was presumably because the technology now being used in oils meant it had better lubricating properties. The problem with that thinking is there were many different oil manufacturers, and not all used the same formula – some being better than others. Therefore, if a poorer brand of oil was being used, there was greater potential for the engine to seize if the 2% mixture instruction was followed.

Whatever the truth was, in April 1961, Lambretta Concessionaires announced that from that date onwards it was safe to run a 2% oil mixture on all new machines. Memorandums were sent out to all Lambretta dealers to instruct old and new owners of the changes, but it wasn't as straightforward as it sounded. It stated that running the Li 125 and 150 on a 2% oil mixture was fine, but the TV 175 must remain at 4%. Not only was it confusing running different models on different oil mixture percentages, it also cast doubt on whether the 2% oil mixture was safe to use in any machine. To avoid confusion, a supplement was attached to the handbook so the customer knew exactly what to do depending on which model they had purchased.

Improvements in both two-stroke oil formulas and engine design by Innocenti continued, but the rule of using a 4% mixture in big-capacity engines remained. After the demise of the TV 175 in 1965, the 200cc models would use the higher percentage mix, including the SX and GP models. Neither Innocenti or Lambretta Concessionaires ever explained why this decision was made. It must be presumed they were never 100% confident that full lubrication could be achieved on the 175cc or 200cc bore only using a 2% mix. In hindsight, it would have been much easier and less confusing if the ruling hadn't been introduced in the first place. Still, because of such fierce rivalry with the competition, it seems any way of gaining an advantage over the opposition had to be taken.

12
The Li/SX Lambretta

The curtain was finally pulled down of the Li 150 in May 1967, ending a decade-long tenure over three different series. It had been the biggest-selling model by a considerable margin, and the series three Slimstyle version had been the backbone of the company's sales during the 1960s. Things were moving on, and its distinct shape started to look somewhat old-fashioned, while the introduction of the SX 150 meant its days were numbered. Even so, it came as a great shock and sad news when it was announced production of it was to cease.

Therefore, it came as a surprise when, a year later, it was being offered to the public once again. The reason for this is there were still a lot of unused frames and bodywork parts left over, so it was offered at a discounted price in an attempt to cash in on the stock. It was described as an Li 150 Special, which used a Li 150 frame but had special side panels. These were the Li type but clip on instead of using handles and translated to an Li 150 with a few bits of different bodywork. Made available in Hawthorn white with the option of either red or blue panels, it proved popular with customers.

One of the reasons for this was its price because, being offered at £179, it was £20 cheaper than the SX 150. By May 1968, it was reported that stocks of it were now exhausted and couldn't continue to be supplied because they had run out of Li 150 engines. To get around this, it was now being offered with an SX 150 engine fitted instead, becoming a sort of Li/SX hybrid, but it would still be called the Li 150 Special.

Doing this meant the cost had to increase slightly, compensating for a current engine being used rather than old stock. The advantage for the customer was a Lambretta that now had the power of an SX 150, which was considerably more expensive than the Li 150 but at a reduced cost.

It was still classed and sold as an Li 150 Special by Lambretta Concessionaires, even though it was a mix of Li and SX components. In today's world of trading standards, that would not be allowed, but back then it was never questioned. It was listed as available by the company as late as October 1968, more than six months after first being offered and 18 months since the demise of the Li 150. It disappeared from pricing schedules soon after, presumably because all stock was now finally exhausted, but there was no press release announcing this fact. Since then, a few examples have shown up, but no official figures as to how many were produced and sold were ever made available.

LAMBRETTA POST BUDGET PRICES - EFFECTIVE 20TH MARCH, 1968.

MODEL.	BASIC.	PURCHASE TAX.	TOTAL.	MAIN DEALERS PROFIT MARGIN	SUB DEALERS PROFIT MARGIN
STARSTREAM	£119. 2. 2.	£30. 17. 4.	£149. 19. 6.	£27. 7. 10.	£23. 5.11.
SUPER STARSTREAM	£127. 1. 0.	£32. 18. 6.	£159. 19. 6.	£29. 4. 4.	£24.17. 1.
150 SPECIAL	£142.18. 8.	£37. 0.10.	£179. 19. 6.	£32.18. 1.	£27.19. 2.
150 SX	£158.16. 4.	£41. 3. 2.	£199. 19. 6.	£36.10. 6.	£31. 1. 4.
200 SX	£191.11.11.	£48. 7. 7.	£239. 19. 6.	£47.17. 11.	£43. 2. 2.
DELIVERY CHARGE	£1. 10. 0.	10. 0.	£2. 0. 0.		

DISCOUNTS :- MAIN DEALER STOCKING 4 MACHINES AND OVER 20% & 3¾% CASH.
EXCEPT SX. 200 NOW 25% C.O.D. (INSTEAD OF 30%) AND NORMAL 20% & 3¾% CASH IF NOT C.O.D.

MAIN DEALER STOCKING LESS THAN 4 MACHINES 17½% & 2½% CASH.
EXCEPT SX. 200 NOW 22½% C.O.D. AND NORMAL 20% & 2½% CASH IF NOT C.O.D.

The manufacturers reserve the right to alter prices and specifications without prior notice.

A price list from March 1968 offering the 150 Special for £20 less than the SX 150

Lambretta

Lambretta Concessionaires Ltd
Lambretta House Purley Way Croydon
CR9 4HD England Phone: 01 686 2499
Telex: 21138 Cables: Lambretta Croydon

N E W S L E T T E R

TO ALL LAMBRETTA DEALERS — NO. 8/68.

Li. 150 Special, now fitted with an SX engine.

Dealers will recall that we were able to introduce the Li. 150 with special side panels and head light at no extra cost.

Unfortunately, stocks of this model are now completely exhausted and it is no longer possible to continue this machine in that particular specification.

However, we are able to install into the standard Li series III frame and body, an SX. 150 engine. Obviously, there has to be a marginal increase in cost.

This does mean that we have had to rationalise our SX. 150 production in favour of this new Li, so please do not allow your stocks to fall to a low level, as difficulties may be experienced for urgent replacements.

This new improved Li. 150 will still be known as the "Li. 150 Special", and will be available in the usual range of colours. Price make-up is as follows :-

BASIC	.....	£149. 5. 9.
P/TAX	.....	£ 38. 13. 9.
TOTAL	.....	£187. 19. 6.

Deliveries start Mid-June, and for all dealers who wish to receive priority, an order Form is enclosed.

Of course it goes (without saying !) like an SX. 150 for £12 less, which we feel your customers will agree is good value for money.

Lambretta Concessionaires Limited,
"Lambretta House",
Purley Way,
Croydon,
Surrey.

17th May, 1968.

In May, two months later, details of the new machine offered with an SX 150 engine but costing slightly more

Lambretta

Lambretta Concessionaires Ltd
Lambretta House Purley Way Croydon
CR9 4HD England Phone: 01 686 2499
Telex: 21138 Cables: Lambretta Croydon

NEWSLETTER.

TO ALL LAMBRETTA DEALERS. NO: 16/68.

In order to bring Dealers up-to-date on our latest colour range we are providing below details of the colour combinations which apply to our various models, together with part numbers covering touch-up paints.

MODEL	COLOUR	2oz. Tin.	½ pt. Tin.	1 pt. Tin.	6oz. Spray.
STARSTREAM	Light Blue	9179	9279	9379	9479
SUPER STARSTREAM	Main Colour - White ...	9169	9269	9369	9469
	Panels - Winchester Blue	9164	9264	9364	9464
	Flame Red	9163	9263	9363	9463
LI.150 SPECIAL	Main Colour - Hawthorn White	9197	9297	9397	9497
	Panels : Scarlet Red ..	9198	9298	9398	N/A.
	Ocean Blue	9199	9299	9399	N/A.
SX.150	All Hawthorn White	9197	9297	9397	9497
	Panels: Scarlet Red ...	9198	9298	9398	N/A.
	Ocean Blue	9199	9299	9399	N/A.
SX.200	All Hawthorn White	9197	9297	9397	9497
	Panels: Lemon	N/A.	9223	N/A.	N/A.
	Lemon & Black	N/A.	9223	N/A.	N/A.
	British Racing Green ..	N/A.	9224	N/A.	N/A.
	Orange	N/A.	9221	N/A.	N/A.
	Lime Green	N/A.	9225	N/A.	N/A.
	Royal Blue	N/A.	9222	N/A.	N/A.
	Black	N/A.	N/A.	N/A.	N/A.
	Poly Blue	N/A.	9292	N/A.	N/A.
	Poly Red	N/A.	9291	N/A.	N/A.
	Poly Copper Pink	N/A.	9289	N/A.	N/A.

NOTE:- Temporarily some of the tins of paint of Hawthorn White are marked as LI/SX.150 OFF WHITE. This is identical to Hawthorn White and when present stocks expire all future tins will be marked Hawthorn White.

1st. October, 1968.

The last known official paperwork for the Li 150 Special from October 1968 shows its colour availability. Note how many different options there were for the SX 200

13
Was tuning a Lambretta prohibited?

When purchasing a brand-new Lambretta, one of its most significant selling points was the warranty. This meant any problems outlined in the policy terms were repaired free of charge. As long as the Lambretta in question was serviced at the correct intervals by an authorised agent, there was nothing to worry about, and the warranty would be honoured. However, any alteration or tampering with the machine, including home repairs and fitting aftermarket products, rendered it void. Despite seeming rather Draconian

Lambretta

Lambretta Concessionaires Ltd
Lambretta House Purley Way Croydon
CR9 4HD England Phone: 01 686 2499
Telex: 21138 Cables: Lambretta Croydon

SPARE PARTS BULLETIN NO. 5

LAMBRETTA PERFORMANCE TUNING IS BIG BUSINESS

The rise in the number of Lambretta owners who are spending considerable sums of money to have their machines tuned or converted has lead to many peculiar developments - some of them more reliable than others - in trade and do-it-yourself tuning. In an attempt to combat some of the problems which have arisen through the use of incorrect spares for these modifications we are now pleased to market special items custom built for the job.

Conversions from 150cc to 175cc

The following pistons are available for the conversion of all 150cc models Li Series to Grand Prix to the very much favoured 175cc capacity. They are all 3-ring Innocenti pistons, manufactured by Borgo and are available in standard size (62mm) and the usual three oversizes. They are made to the same high standards as normal Lambretta pistons to ensure that no problems due to incorrect coefficient of expansion can occur.

Piston rings, gudgeon pins and circlips are readily available as spares as these are identical to those of the TV 175 Series 3.

Please order using the following part numbers :

Standard Size	62mm.	41912310
First Oversize	62.2mm	41912320
Second Oversize	62.4mm	41912330
Third Oversize	62.6mm	41912340

Normal Lambretta boring tolerances apply for these pistons and all are offered at the special nett price of 27/6d - retail price £2.1.3d.

Continued/- - - -

Announcing in October 1969 that Lambretta tuning is big business and, therefore, the company will now officially stock certain performance upgrades

today, this was a standard rule across the industry at the time and was widely regarded as perfectly acceptable.

Lambretta Concessionaires were very strict about the warranty, especially when it came to tuning or any alteration to the engine. Any changes made in this area by the customer would immediately void the warranty, and dealers were constantly reminded that the policy should be pointed out to a customer when they purchased a brand-new machine. The practice of engine modification became more prevalent in the 1960s but the company continued to take a particularly dim view of it – even something as simple as fitting a different exhaust.

By the end of the decade, Lambretta tuning was big business and certainly among the younger generation of owners. Shops that catered for them began to spring up, with many owners having their engines considerably tuned. They didn't seem worried about losing their warranty, and it must be remembered that many owners were using machines where the warranty had naturally expired anyway, so it didn't matter to them. By this time, Lambretta Concessionaires had seen the shift towards tuning, so the company began offering specific products to boost the engine's performance, in other words, back-door tuning.

The commonest option was fitting a 22mm carburettor, which had been introduced on the Grand

- 2 -

22mm Carburettor Kits for GT and SX Models.

This kit includes all parts necessary to fit a 22mm Dell'Orto Carburettor to GT and SX200 models. A full instruction sheet is enclosed with each kit.

A noticeable increase in performance should be gained with the advantages of a proper air filter and ready availability of spare parts plus complete tractability.

Contents:	1	-	00412485	Carburettor
	1	-	22211004	Inlet Manifold
	1	-	22016021	Air Hose
	1	-	19916160	Clamp for air hose
	1	-	19015031	Inner throttle cable

Please order using part number 00412100, the retail price of the complete kit is £7.17.6d less 20%.

We are sure that every dealer is aware of the fact that tuning of the kind described above is expressly excluded by the terms of the Warranty of the vehicle manufacturer.

ETA/LG/COM:
October, 1969.

Page 2 of the document offers other tuning items while underneath mentioning that if such items are fitted, the warranty on a machine will be void

Lambretta

Lambretta Concessionaires Ltd
Lambretta House Purley Way Croydon
CR9 4HD England Phone: 01 686 2499
Telex: 21138 Cables: Lambretta Croydon

SPARE PARTS BULLETIN NO. 6

TO: All Lambretta Dealers

1) THE FIRST LAMBRETTA MANUAL OF PERFORMANCE TUNING AND CONVERSION.

We are very pleased to be able to introduce a specially produced 60 page illustrated booklet covering performance tuning, available conversions and many other subjects which the enthusiast needs to know. This booklet has been prepared by our own Technical Department and trade experts. Contents are easy to follow by diagrams, photographs and will be nationally advertised to coincide with this bulletin. Demand will be great - deliveries are anticipated mid-December and you are requested to place your firm order NOW:

Lambretta Manual of Performance Tuning and Conversion - Part Number 10201 - Retail Price 12/6d less 20% trade discount.

2) You will recall our last bulletin introduced to you the availability of Carburettor Tuning Kits and Oversize Pistons now available from our Spare Parts Stores to assist in improving the overall performance on certain models. To date we are very pleased with the demand this announcement has created. Many dealers have taken advantage of this special offer and to ensure that you are aware of this availability we are detailing below the relevant part numbers and prices :-

22mm Carburettor Kit for GT/SX models - Part No. 00412100 - Retail Price £7.17.6d less 20% - consisting of :

1	-	00412485	-	Carburettor
1	-	22211004	-	Inlet Manifold
1	-	22016021	-	Air Hose
1	-	19916160	-	Clamp for Air Hose
1	-	19015031	-	Inner Throttle Cable

Conversions from 150cc to 175cc

Standard Size Piston	62mm	41912310
First Oversize "	62.2mm	41912320
Second Oversize "	62.4mm	41912330
Third Oversize "	62.6mm	41912340

The above pistons are priced at special nett £1.7.6d - Retail Price £2.1.3d.

Continued/. . . .

Two months later, another press release on the subject, this time for the new tuning manual

Prix in 1969 and was now being offered on models that only had the 20mm option. Also, rebore kits became available, allowing the capacity of 150cc engines to be increase to 175cc. While this sounded good, it was in fact a rather callous attempt at cashing in on this new trend. On the one hand, Lambretta Concessionaires were offering tuning products, but at the same time, they warned that if the products mentioned were fitted, the warranty would be void. Theoretically, they were promoting tuning of the Lambretta but still saying it was prohibited.

The book that was a must for all Lambretta owners who wanted better performance from the engine regardless of the warranty terms and conditions

Even more outrageous was introducing a book with the sole purpose of improving the performance of your Lambretta – anything from tuning the engine to upgrading the brakes. It included pages and pages of information with the sole purpose of making your Lambretta faster. By the time of the book's introduction in December 1969, the Grand Prix was available in all three variants: 125, 150 and 200cc. Now, an owner could purchase the book, modify the machine they had just bought, and instantly void its warranty. Not only were Lambretta Concessionaires able to write off warranties on new machines, but they were also making money from the book that was helping them do it.

Owners, it seems, weren't too bothered as the racing scene was going into overdrive and new machines were being thrashed on tracks up and down the country once run in. Tuning a Lambretta wasn't prohibited by the factory any more – it was encouraged. It's just that it came with certain conditions, but evidently the young generation of owners weren't the slightest bit worried.

The book itself which was so successful it required a second print not long after launch due to its popularity. It was compiled and written by Ken Hurlingshaw, who worked for Lambretta Concessionaires and had the full backing of Peter Agg to produce it. Another twist in the plot was the drawings used within it. They were done by none other than Tony Tessier, who had competed in the Milan Taranto and Moto Giro races for the factory team and built the Lambrettair hovercraft. It showed some talented individuals were working within and indirectly for the company and were one of the driving forces behind the Lambretta success story in the UK.

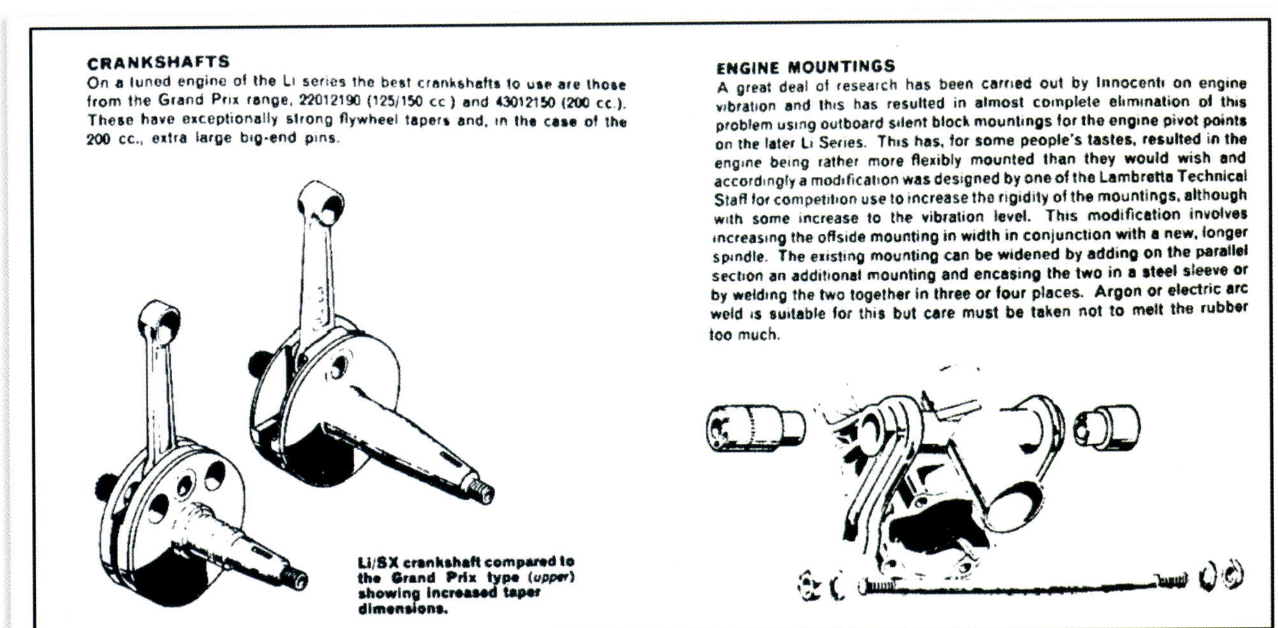

Examples of the drawings inside done by Tony Tessier

14 There was no such thing as the Lambretta series one

By the mid-1950s, Innocenti was dominating the scooter market, but in order to keep ahead they needed to keep improving the Lambretta. At the time, the LD had been available for several years through different marks but needed replacing. Until now, all models had been shaft-driven and relatively low powered. Rivals such as the Vespa were surging ahead with their GS model in terms of performance and speed, so Innocenti needed to do something about it.

Development was well underway for two new models which would be totally different from all those that preceded them and would propel the Lambretta forward.

They boasted a new horizontal layout engine which would be more powerful and would give better all-around performance by using a chain drive connected to a four-speed gearbox. Improvements were made to the chassis too, along with bigger 10in wheels, improving the handling along with greater braking power and better suspension.

Added to all this was a total revamp of the styling, which made it more modern-looking and proved the Lambretta was still the market leader. The models were named the Li, available in 125 and 150cc variants, and the TV, which would be 175cc. Li stood for Lambretta Innocenti, while TV was short for Turismo Veloce, which translated to 'fast tourer', appropriate enough as it could reach speeds in excess of 60mph.

That was it, nothing else – they were just called the Li 125, Li 150 and TV 175. The TV came out in late 1957, followed by the Li range a few months later. Even though Innocenti had made an enormous stride ahead, they were not prepared to rest on their laurels and began developing the next generation of machines. It was decided to upgrade the existing models rather than something completely different, like the transition from the LD. When they were introduced in 1959, they were called the Li and TV second series, and it was only then that the 'series one' label retrospectively came into use, the name wasn't changed, the initial release models were just referred to that way. Advertising and instruction manuals, in fact, anything never mentioned them as series one because they never existed as such.

The new Lambretta TV 175 is advertised as nothing else

The same when the Li models came out a few months later

Even equipment manufacturers only referred to it as the new Li

All literature regarding handbooks or technical never referred to them as series one while they were in production

15
What was the LD Mk IV?

The last variant of the LD was the Mark III, which finished production in 1958 when the Li and TV models superseded it. This signalled the end of the shaft drive Lambretta as the company introduced mechanically improved and more modern designs. The new models were a tremendous advancement, making the LD look very dated almost overnight and because so many had been sold, it meant

Lambretta DEALER

Lambretta
Newsletter

Lambretta SERVICE AGENT

To: All Lambretta Dealers. No ...... 15/59.

NEW MODEL - LD.125 c.c. Mark IV.
PRICE - £129.19.6. inc. P.T.
LAUNCHING DATE - 22nd July, 1959

As a result of repeated requests by Lambretta Dealers for a Lambretta scooter which could be retailed at about £130., we are happy to announce our intention to introduce a new model LD.125, built at the new £5.-million Innocenti Factory in France.

Consistent with our policy when introducing new models, spare parts are immediately available. For ease of identification when ordering spares and other items relating to this new machine, it will be known as the LD.125 Mk.IV.

We give below further details of this new model :-

Price. Basic .... £ 107. 15. 0.
Purchase Tax .... 22. 4. 6.
£ 129. 19. 6.

The pillion seat and spare wheel are extra.

Colour. Two-tone Grey.

Delivery. Orders will be taken in strict rotation with priority - if necessary - being given to those of our Dealers holding our Official Service Agency Appointment.

Availability. This model will remain available (subject to demand) until at least the end of 1960.

Announcing the New LD MK IV in May 1959, which was the old French LD 125 with a different name to make it sound better

The advert looked good, but it was an outdated machine by the time of its launch

Offered at £130-4s, it was cheap enough, and many customers were keen to grab this Lambretta bargain

Another advertising ploy to make it sound cheaper was to offer it at 124 guineas, which was £130-4s, so there was no difference in the price

Lambretta DEALER

Lambretta Newsletter

Lambretta SERVICE AGENT

To: All Lambretta Dealers 38/59

LD.125 Mark IV

As these new models are now reaching the first Agents to place orders we should mention that, in many cases, we are despatching these machines complete with pillion seat, spare wheel with disc and bracket. We feel that it is wiser to deliver the machines with these Accessories fitted, rather than hold them in our warehouse until such time as we have staff available to remove the pillion seats and spare wheels, should some Agents so require.

Nevertheless it is almost certain that all our Agents will regard the price of these machines, with Accessories, as even more competitive than that of the naked machine.

Prices are as follows :-

LD.125 Mark IV - Basic	£ 107. 15. 0.
Purchase Tax	22. 4. 6.
	£ 129. 19. 6.
Pillion seat - Basic	£ 2. 18. 11.
Purchase Tax	12. 2.
	£ 3. 11. 1.
Spare wheel with disc and bracket - Basic	£ 4. 5. 0.
Purchase Tax	17. 6.
	£ 5. 2. 6.

Therefore for £138. 13. 1d. the customer purchases a machine with :-

Steering lock,
Pillion seat,
Spare wheel,
Spare wheel bracket and disc,
Lockable glove box and mirror.

30th July, 1959

Lambretta Concessionaires Limited,
Beverley Works,
Kingston by Pass, London, S.W.20.

To cash in even more, a pillion seat and spare wheel were offered as extras, putting another £8-13s on the sale price

there was a huge second-hand market for them.

While it was sad to see the LD go, the world had moved on and it soon became forgotten. However, it had a renaissance thanks to the requirement for a cheaper model. By mid-1959, the series two was in full production, and in the UK customers couldn't get enough of them. As quickly as the showrooms could be filled, they were being emptied as the Lambretta reached its peak in terms of sales in the UK. Selling them was a straightforward task, but dealers reported that they were getting enquiries for something cheaper. At the time, the Li 125 was the most affordable model, coming in at £157, but Lambretta Concessionaires was not going to drop the price. There was no need to because they sold with such ease, so it would have been counterproductive.

It must be remembered that there were now hundreds of dealers across the country, and any price change had to be reflected across the board. A significant price drop of the Li 125 would cost the company a considerable amount of money, so it would never happen. Also, by now, many Li 125s had been sold at the full price, and dropping it would disgruntle loyal customers, something Peter Agg would never do. Even so, he was a businessman and saw a potential solution to the problem.

His idea was to announce that a new model, the LD Mk IV, would be made available to dealers. It came as something of a surprise that a model long since forgotten about was once again being made available, and dealers were very sceptical about it. It may have been outdated, but coming in with a price of £127 it was cheaper than any other Lambretta by a considerable margin. Agg was sure a lower price tag would lure those who wanted a bargain and he wasn't wrong, with LD Mk IVs being snapped up so fast they couldn't keep up with demand.

The question remained: what were these customers actually buying, because Innocenti had stopped production of the LD a while back. The answer was a French LD made at the Lambretta factory at Troyes in central France. This had been in production for several years, and there was still a market for it there, but it was an old model. The Mk IV sounded like something new when, in fact, it wasn't. It was another of Peter Agg's schemes that made it sound enticing. Again, this was in the days when trading standards didn't seem to worry too much about the devious ways in which companies advertised their products. With customers grabbing such a bargain, they didn't seem to mind either that what they were buying wasn't really an LD Mk IV. It never existed as such, apart from being a clever marketing ploy.

16
What happened to the Lambretta Amphiscooter?

Of all the wacky scooter inventions, the Lambretta Amphiscooter has to be one of the strangest. It was the idea of Doug Bedford helped by Rex White, who worked in the technical department of Lambretta Concessionaires; they had the idea of making a Lambretta that could travel on both land and water. At the height of the mid-1960s, when inventions for tomorrow were all the rage, the goal was to solve the traffic problems of inner-city living. It would never be a practical solution, but nonetheless, Bedford was determined to prove it was possible.

Close to the factory in Croydon was a company that made plastic floats, and he believed it was possible to fit one on either side of a machine so that it would float on water. The Lambretta in question was a J 125 mainly because it was much lighter than the series three models and stood a better chance of floating. Also, its vertical engine stood a better chance of staying clear of the water as opposed to the traditional horizontal engine layout. The floats required were huge – longer than the machine itself and very wide. The idea was to fix them onto struts mounted to the frame that could be folded up when on the road and down when in the water. This was crucial because they had to retract for road use to prove the idea was possible; otherwise, the machine would be too wide.

The other problem was getting the float height just right. The rear wheel had to be immersed so it could drive the scooter in the water, but the exhaust pipe had to be high enough so it could vent the engine gases into the air. The front mount went under the frame but at the back it required an elaborate mounting to go around the frame, since the rear wheel was in the way of mounting it underneath. Once he was happy that the height was correct, all Doug had to do now was work out how to propel it through the water. The

Co-inventor and builder Doug Bedford proudly salutes the success of the Lambretta Amphiscooter during its debut at Brighton in 1965

Sir Donald Cambpell seen here putting it through its paces at Lake Coniston

Having booked it at so many events, Lambretta Concessionaires PR manager Bob Wilkinson finally tried it out for himself

Lambretta

Lambretta Concessionaires Ltd
Lambretta House Purley Way Croydon
CR9 4HD England Phone: 01 686 2499
Telex: 21138 Cables: Lambretta Croydon

STOP PRESS

FOR IMMEDIATE RELEASE

FLOATING SCOOTER ON MANCHESTER'S CANAL

Is this the Answer to Road Conjestion?

Permission has today been granted by the Manchester Ship Canal Co. for a floating scooter to make the journey on the Bridgewater Canal from Sale, Cheshire to Longford Bridge, Manchester on Tuesday, 2nd April.

The aquascooter, a Lambretta specially converted with fold down floats and a unique motor which drives it along at 4 knots on water or 50 m.p.h. on the road, is the brain child of 40 year old Doug Bedford, a York scooter engineer.

Commenting on his unusal invention, Mr. Bedford said today: "It is surely the answer to road conjestion. I just drive along the road until I meet a hold up - then its down with the floats and into the nearest canal to continue my journey."

After leaving the water in Manchester, Mr. Bedford will drive his Lambretta by road to Belle Vue where it will be on display during the International Motorcycle and Cycle Show.

Picture shows the aquascooter inventor, Doug Bedford (left) with fellow designer, Rex White, during proving trials.

Further information from:
Robert K. Wilkinson,
Lambretta Concessionaires Ltd.

26th March, 1968.

CHAIRMAN: A JAMES AGG
MANAGING DIRECTOR: P JAMES AGG
DIRECTOR: EDNA M CALDER

One of the press launches from 1968 saw the Amphiscooter travelling down the Manchester shipping canal. Over two years after it was first launched, wear and tear was taking its toll on the float mounts, which gave way soon after – causing it to sink to the bottom of Mallory Park lake

solution was to fix a plate to the rear wheel with several paddle blades that stuck out sideways. They had limited room, measuring only a couple of inches wide and were attached to an outer disc to strengthen them, the visual appearance being reminiscent of a water wheel. These blades provided enough drive to move the scooter in the water while still allowing it to be driven on the road.

Once tested, the machine was prepared and had the inscription 'Lambretta Amphi-Scooter' written along the side of the floats. It debuted at the 1965 Brighton Motorcycle Show and became the most prominent attraction there. Realising it had huge PR potential, Bob Wilkinson was determined to take full advantage of it. From that moment onwards, the Amphiscooter became a star in its own right, making appearances everywhere: on the seafront at Brighton before doing a demonstration in the sea, down the Thames passing by the Houses of Parliament and so on. It was filmed by Pathe News and appeared on Blue Peter, and as for magazines, there were almost constant articles on it for well over two years.

Bob remembers: "We took it and used it just about anywhere and everywhere there was water … We certainly got our money's worth out of it." While the fabrication of it was made as strong as possible over time, the wear and tear from frequently going in and out of the water took its toll. "I remember it being on a lake, and finally, the supports on one side gave way and it sank,". The lake was at Mallory Park with Doug Saunders on it. Though he did his best to save it under the water, it went down and that was the end of it. It is unclear whether it was ever recovered so, just like the Titanic, perhaps it still sits at the bottom of the water, waiting to be rediscovered one day.

17
Why didn't the twin-cylinder Lambretta go into production?

Shortly after the launch of the SX 200 in 1966, a proposal was put forward to develop new ideas for the Lambretta. One of these was given the title Project 137 and was centred around the engine. The concept was for a twin-cylinder engine that would have more power. Using two 100cc cylinders opposing each other would not only improve acceleration and top speed but would also make power delivery much smoother.

Creating it was well within the capabilities of Innocenti, but it would still require a big budget to achieve. This was because it was an entirely different design and would therefore require new tooling.

Many other developments, such as a more responsive disc brake and possibly a bigger wheel diameter, were also worked on. A prototype was built, and an extensive test programme was begun to ensure the engine worked flawlessly, ironing out any possible faults. The base machine chosen was, in fact, an SX 150, and fitting the new engine into the frame meant a huge amount of fabrication. With two carburettors to feed the engine, a central airbox had to be installed, which meant the toolbox had to be sacrificed to make room. A rather crude-looking but adequate box section exhaust was also made, fitting width-ways on the underside of the frame. It didn't matter because it was a testbed. If the concept work was approved, the cosmetic side could be ironed out at a later date.

By the summer of 1967, the prototype had been rigorously tested and performed flawlessly. How secret the project was being kept at the time is anyone's guess, but on a trip to the factory from the UK, Mike Karslake spotted it. He recalled: "I saw a Lambretta being put through its paces, which was common inside the factory's vast road network ... This one sounded different though, and I thought this is no normal Lambretta." With the machine finally parked up, he went over to inspect it, noticed the two exhaust pipes underneath, and realised it was a twin-cylinder Lambretta. Once back at the factory in the UK, he told Peter Agg what he had seen, and Mike remembers Peter telling him: "No, you didn't." In other words, keep your mouth shut about it.

It didn't matter because rumours were beginning to circulate among the company's top brass that Innocenti was about to launch something special. There was virtually no coverage anywhere, which seemed strange considering it would be groundbreaking and create huge media interest. By 1968, a second prototype had been built, and much had improved on the first. This was the one ready to go into production – all it needed now was approval. To make that happen, Innocenti needed to guarantee sales of it, which could only be done by getting orders from Lambretta Concessionaires because they were their biggest customer.

The SX 200 had fared okay in Italy, but Italian customers hadn't long had access to a 200cc Lambretta because the TV 200 that proceeded it was an export-only model. The primary market for a machine like this was the UK, and Innocenti wanted Lambretta Concessionaires to place a big order to guarantee their investment if it went into production, and this is where the plan unravelled. There were several factors that

Weeks after being discovered at the Innocenti factory in Milan the twin-cylinder Lambretta revealed its secrets for the first time

This was the first prototype machine built and it didn't have any side panels. The makeshift dual airbox took up a lot of the space where the toolbox once sat

The extended frame piece to possibly take a bigger wheel or move the engine position

played a part in Peter Agg's decision. Undoubtedly, the twin cylinder scooter would be more expensive to produce and, therefore, would need to have a higher price tag. By now, an SX 200 would cost the customer £239, which was at the top end of what could realistically be asked. Though younger people were prepared to pay for outstanding performance, many still wanted a Lambretta just to go to work on.

This was pointed out by sales manager Maurice Knight, who saw the threat from lightweight motorcycles beginning to come over from Japan. That was the competition, and offering better weather protection was what meant most; that was what would give them an advantage. Big performance wasn't required, and not only would a twin cylinder be more expensive, but it most likely would require more servicing again, costing the customer yet more money.

Another reason was the recent devaluation of the pound by then-Prime Minister Harold Wilson. Peter Agg detested him because although the measure was intended to make exports out of the UK cheaper, it conversely meant that bringing goods in became more expensive. The result was a 15% increase in the cost of a Lambretta overnight when it happened in November 1967.

By mid-1968, purchase tax was also steadily rising along with inflation as the Government failed to improve the economy. The fear was that by the time an order from Innocenti had arrived, it might cost even more, a problem they already had with the models they stocked. The risk was too great to take on financially, and with the question being raised of whether it was even needed, Agg wasn't prepared to commit to an order – certainly not on the scale Innocenti needed if the venture was to prove worthwhile. Once that decision was made, Innocenti had to take the risk on their own and, with no guarantee it would sell, pulled the plug. There was never any question regarding the performance or reliability of the twin cylinder Lambretta – if anything it was a fantastic piece of engineering. What killed it was the production cost at a time of great financial uncertainty. Had it come about a couple of years earlier, Lambretta Concessionaires may have been better positioned to gamble on it. The only reminder of the project now is the two prototypes discarded at the factory and discovered in the 1980s.

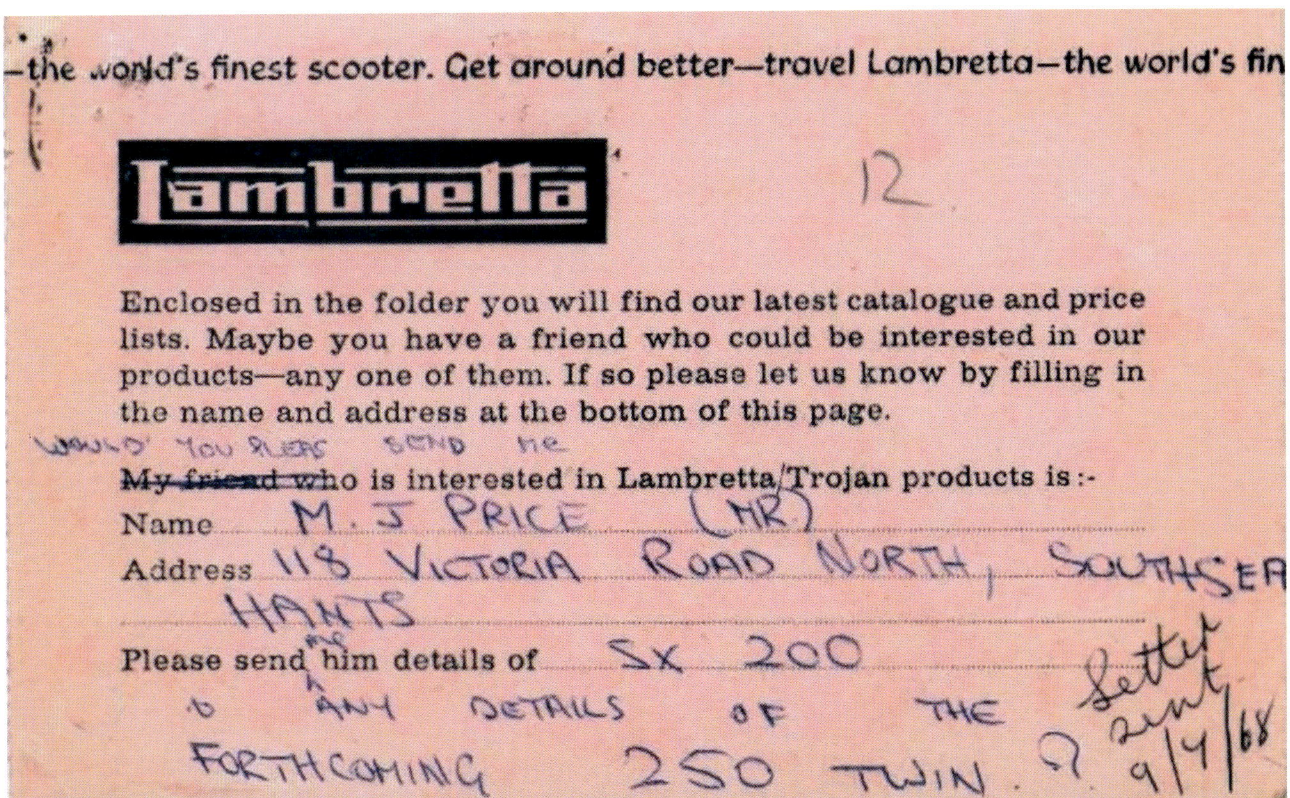

–the world's finest scooter. Get around better—travel Lambretta—the world's fin

Lambretta 12

Enclosed in the folder you will find our latest catalogue and price lists. Maybe you have a friend who could be interested in our products—any one of them. If so please let us know by filling in the name and address at the bottom of this page.

WOULD YOU PLEASE SEND ME ~~My friend who~~ is interested in Lambretta/Trojan products is :-

Name M. J PRICE (MR)

Address 118 VICTORIA ROAD NORTH, SOUTHSEA HANTS

Please send me him details of SX 200 & ANY DETAILS OF THE FORTHCOMING 250 TWIN. ?

letter sent 9/7/68

While no official paperwork has ever surfaced, this return slip for information on models dated July 9, 1968 has. It requests details on the forthcoming 250 twin with a question mark

18
Was the SX 200 intended to look different?

The decision to produce a 200cc Lambretta had undoubtedly been the correct one. It may have taken pressure from the UK to persuade Innocenti to build it, but the success of the TV 200 was undeniable. There was, however, one problem with it because being an export-only model, customers in Innocenti's home market of Italy were unable to obtain it. There hadn't been too many grumblings though, because the TV 175 had constantly been available there, but the time had now come for the 200cc Lambretta to be introduced. The easiest way to do so was to create a new model that would have type approval in Italy, and that's what was done.

This meant that Innocenti would have exclusive rights to the new machine, unlike the deal they had struck with Peter Agg when the TV 200 was introduced. While he and Lambretta Concessionaires would not have exclusivity on this new 200cc model, he wasn't bothered in the slightest. For him, it was vindication that he was right in pursuing it in the first place and would be allowed to sell it. If anything, he was looking forward to it as it was bound to be an improvement on the TV 200. While the TV 200 was generally fine, certain engine parts needed development to iron out one or two weak points.

The most notable improvement was a reduction in vibration from the engine, which was achieved by creating a better balance with the top end. The crank end float was changed from the top end to the bottom end, and with better balance of the crank, there was less vibration. Along with a different cylinder design and revised barrel porting, the result was a much smoother power delivery. The other significant change was to the gearbox, which in the TV 200 was rather long and meant it could struggle in 4th gear. The TV 175 gearbox was used instead, resulting in a closer gap between the 3rd and the 4th gears. The only downside of all these engine modifications was a slightly reduced top speed – but there was better acceleration, so it was a compromise in one area but an improvement in another.

In October 1965, production of the TV 200 ceased, ready for the introduction of the new model, which would start in January 1966. It was to be called the SX 200, which stood for Special Extra and, apart from

An early UK press shot of the SX 200 with the body styling we are accustomed to

the engine modifications, would also be cosmetically different. The frame and chassis would be the same, as would the braking and suspension. It was the change to the styling which would be seen as an improvement, offering a more modern look, because the Li 150 Special, TV 175, and TV 200 all had the same bodywork. The most notable feature of this was the side panels, which incorporated a different profile with a more prominent raised lip along the length. It featured a V-shaped flash with three prongs, and for the only time on a 200cc model, the number 200 was included.

It has always been accepted that all the new designs and features present in the production model SX 200 were just as they were intended to be. However, after researching in more depth, there is evidence to suggest

LIST OF PARTS FOR THE GT 200 AND
SPECIAL X 200 WHICH DIFFER FROM THE TV 175

Part No	Refer to	Description	Model
00412209		Main Jet 108	GT
00412352		Carburetter SHI/20	Common
00412353		Pilot Jet 48	Common
00412407		Main Jet 103	SX
00611097		Speedometer M.P.H.	SX
19518010		Exhaust Pipe	SX
19550150		Motif 'Special'	SX
19610060		Silentblock	SX
19610160		Crankcase	Common
19611003		Cylinder Head Gasket	GT
19611004		Induction Manifold	Common
19611012		Long stud for Induction Manifold	Common
19611017		Gasket for Induction Manifold	Common
19611040	19611050	Cylinder assembly	SX
19611030	19611060	Cylinder assembly	GT
19612018		Gudgeon Pin	SX
19612150		Crankshaft	SX
19612310		Piston assembly 66.0	Common
612320		Piston assembly 66.2	Common
19612330		Piston assembly 66.4	Common
19612340		Piston assembly 66.6	Common
19616022		Spring clips for rubber induction hose	SX
19618060		Silencer	GT
19620015		Clutch Spring	Common
19630001		Gear group	GT
19630003		First Gear	GT
19630004		Second Gear	GT
19630005		Third Gear	GT
19630006		Fourth Gear	GT
19630029		Kickstart Pedal	SX
19650170		Motif 'Lambretta'	SX
19650190		Motif 'X 200'	SX
19650200		Motif 'TV 200'	GT
19655072	19955093	Rear Flash 'TV 200'	GT
19655076		Panel Flash LH	SX
19655077		Panel Flash RH	SX
19655180		Side Panel LH	SX
19655190		Side Panel RH	SX
19912011		Washers for Gudgeon Pin	Common
19955093		Rear Flash 'Lambretta'	SX
42010005		Cylinder Base Gasket	Common
42011002		Cylinder Head	Common
42011003		Cylinder Head Gasket	SX
42012018		Gudgeon Pin	GT
42012024		Piston Ring 66.0	Common
42012025		Piston Ring 66.2	Common
42012026		Piston Ring 66.4	Common
42012027		Piston Ring 66.6	Common
42912150		Crankshaft	GT

Also refer to Supplement No. 4 to the Slimstyle Spare Parts Book

The only paperwork which exists to show similarities and differences between engine components on the TV and SX 200

KEYS

The sets of keys supplied with your scooter are for the main light switch in the centre of the handlebar facing the driver, see fig. 3, for the steering lock fitted under the left hand of the handlebar and for the luggage box situated in the central front rib of the frame (fig. 4). Each key has a number stamped on it and the same number is stamped on the lock or switch itself, so that in the case of loss, a remplacement can be obtained by quoting the appropriate number.

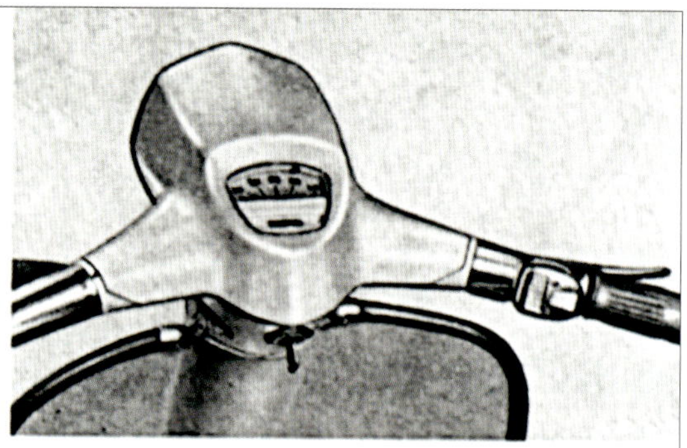

Fig. 3

Fig. 4

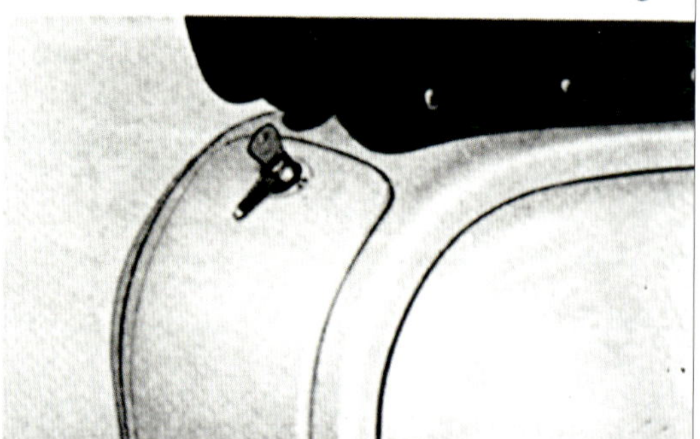

Inside the instruction manual for the SX 200, the hi/lo horn switch is shown in white, and some early ones were known to have that colour fitted

TECHNICAL CHARACTERISTICS

Engine	single cylinder two-stroke
Total capacity	198 cc
Compression ratio	7 : 1
Maximum effective power	11 HP at 5.500 rpm
Gear box	4 speeds
Clutch	multi-disc in oil bath
Primary transmission	by means of chain
Rear wheel	fixed on axle of gear box
Top speed	approx. 70 mph
Fuel tank capacity	1.9 gallons
Front brake	disc type
Rear brake	drum type
Frame construction	in large bore steel tubing
Body work	in steel pressings with removable side panels
Front suspension	trailing forks
Rear suspension	swinging arm
Dry weight	242 lbs
Overall length	71"
Maximum height at head lamp	3' 4"
Maximum width at handle bar	27"

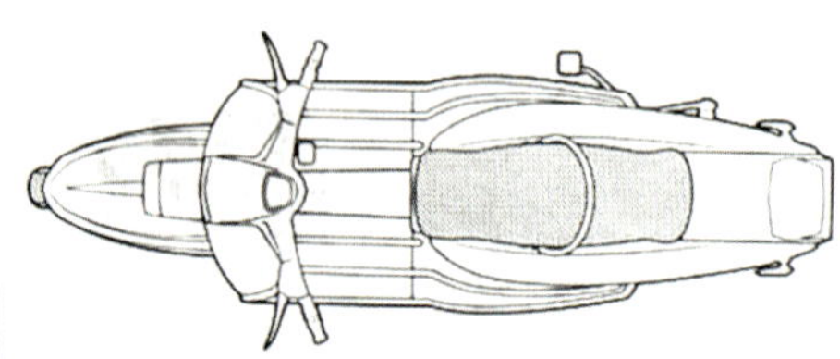

INNOCENTI

MILANO ROMA NEW YORK PARIGI LONDRA CARACAS DUSSELDORF

There wasn't a great deal of promotional paperwork made available, but this specification page from a leaflet shows the correct side panels

otherwise. One area is with the engine, as some parts were used on the TV 200 that appeared on the SX 200. Most notable was the engine casing, even though the number stamp on the top was changed, and the cylinder head which appeared on early examples. Like any crossover model where components are interchangeable, there is always the possibility that leftover stock will be used rather than thrown away. The evidence to back this up isn't easy to find because Innocenti didn't release a parts manual for the TV 200 because it was an export model. The only literature that exists is from Lambretta Concessionaires, and during TV 200 production, it was sporadic at best.

One document that does exist was released in 1966 and lists components that differ between each model and those that are common. This proves that some items mentioned had identical part numbers and, therefore, were the same, certainly during the early production of the SX 200 until the stock of those parts was exhausted. The reason for mentioning this is that the cosmetic side throws up the biggest mystery and still cannot be explained.

To highlight crossover differences, a good example is the high/low and horn switch. This had used white buttons on the TV 200 and did so on the early SX 200 models, proof of which is seen in the SX 200

The standard colour for the switch was black

handbook, which clearly shows a white switch. Again, this was most likely to get rid of old stock, and when exhausted, it was changed to black, the colour it was always associated with.

All of this strengthens the case that at the beginning of SX 200 production, anything was possible regarding how it was produced and what was fitted to it. However, the homologation certificate for the machine exposes something that can't be explained. Part of the requirement is side views of the machine and its dimensions. This clearly shows it with a TV 200-style side panel, not the one we all associate the SX 200 with. The certificate is dated October 14, 1965, less than three months before production started. Was this the originally intended side panel design to be used? If not, it didn't leave Innocenti much time to change it, and there are no additions or amendments to the certificate that show that another side panel had been approved in its place.

To confuse matters even more, it could be presumed that it was a case of getting rid of old stock, such as the components already highlighted. That theory doesn't stand up because the Li 150, Special, 125 Special, and SX 150 all used the same side panel design, so it continued to be produced up until 1969, therefore blowing the old stock theory out of the water. No SX 200 has ever been reported or found featuring this side panel design, but there is clear evidence to show the design was approved, and so, at present, the resolution to this Lambretta myth remains inconclusive.

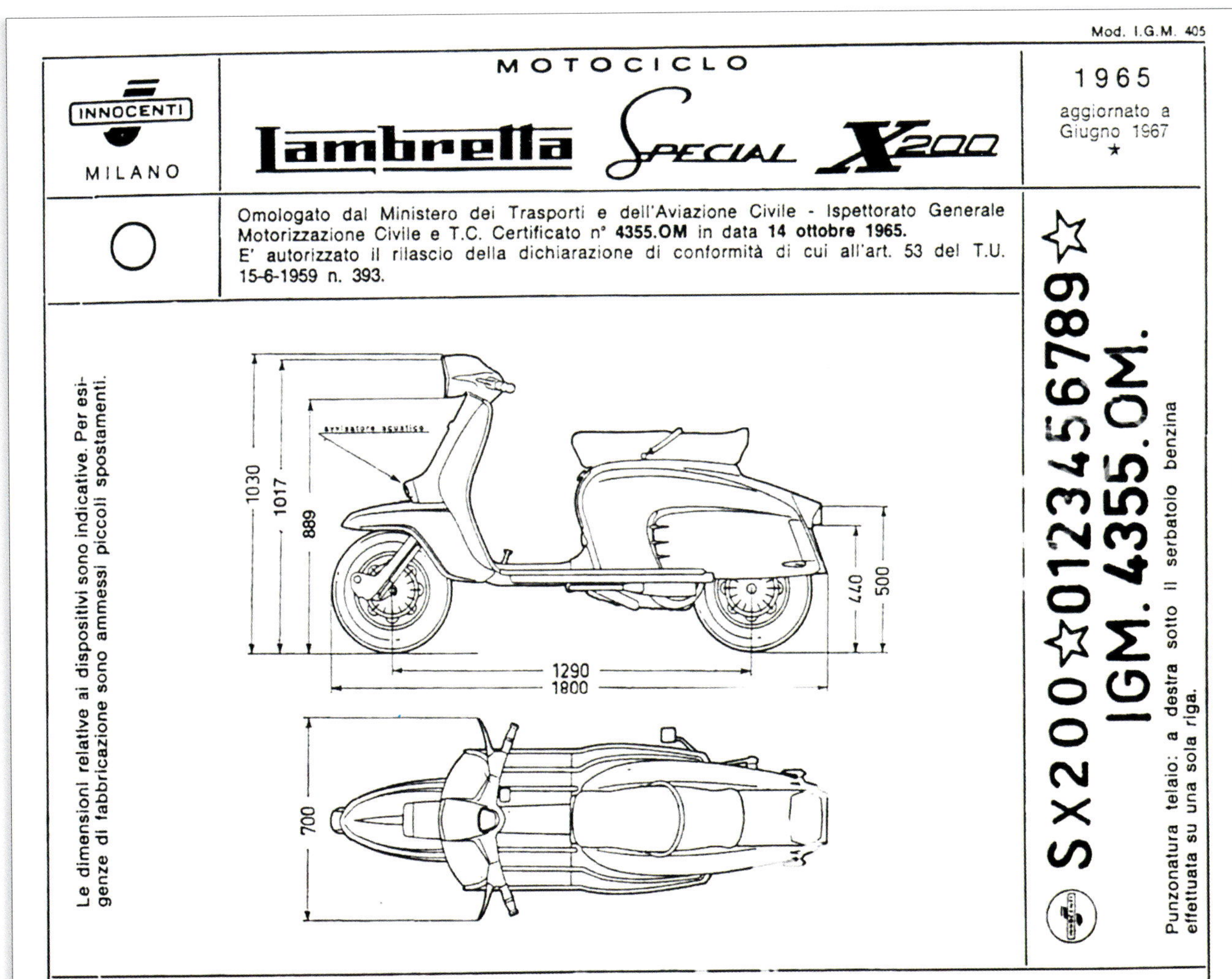

The homologation certificate for the SX 200, dated October 1965, clearly shows the old-style side panels fitted to the TV 200 for approval. This was only three months before it went into production

19
The SX 150 was sold at the same time as the Grand Prix 150

While the SX 200 was undoubtedly regarded as the world's finest scooter, according to Innocenti, its partner in the series was the real unsung hero. The SX 150 was not only the most powerful 150cc Lambretta when introduced and by a considerable margin but was also very important in keeping the brand alive. By the time of its introduction in the autumn of 1966, it soon became the only 150cc Lambretta available with the Li 150 being phased out a few months later. While the SX 200 would take all the glory with its stunning design and powerful delivery, the SX 150 would balance the books.

Its somewhat subdued launch and coverage in the press were more because a 150cc Lambretta had been in the model lineup since the 1950s, so it was taken for granted that one would be available. Regardless, production of the SX 150 came at a turbulent time for the company, with sales declining in general and towards the end of its tenure when strikes were having a considerable effect. Without it, the company could have been in a more dire financial position, so it became the saviour of the Lambretta brand.

With a new model looming in the shape of the Grand Prix, its days were numbered, so when production stopped in January 1969 it was presumed that was the end of it. However, a huge stock of SX 150s was still available, and many of them were destined for the UK. There were enough for Lambretta Concessionaires to keep offering it throughout 1969, and it was available at the same time as the Grand Prix 150, which had been introduced in March, some nine months earlier. Its price was dropped slightly to compensate for the fact that it was now an older model and for customers still being tempted to buy it.

What was more significant was the news in December that not only would its availability be finished in the UK, but a 125 model would replace it. That would be the Grand Prix 125. Though the press release stated it was equal in performance, that wasn't quite true as it had slightly less power. Though its days were numbered, in truth the SX 150 was indeed available at the same time as the Grand Prix 150 and showed what an important Lambretta design it was; in many people's eyes, one of the greatest.

Press releases in Italy were minimal regarding the SX 150; however, it did feature in one of the most defining Lambretta images ever taken

In the UK, it was responsible for the SX appeal campaign thought up by Bob Wilkinson and pushing to the edge of what was regarded as acceptable

LAMBRETTA SCOOTER PRICES – FROM 1st NOV. 1969.

MODEL	BASIC	P.T.	TOTAL	Main Dealer Profit Margin		Sub-Dealer Profit Margin	
				C.O.D.	30 DAYS	C.O.D.	30 DAYS
75S Vega	£112.16. 4.	£29. 3. 8.	£142. 0. 0.	As per Newsletter No 9/69 dated 11.6.69.			
75SL Cometa	£121. 3. 0.	£31. 7. 0.	£152.10. 0.				
150 SX	£143. 7. 6.	£41.12. 3.	£184.19. 6.	£31. 0. 0.	£27. 0. 0.	£26. 0. 0.	£23.10. 0.
150 GP	£159.16. 9.	£46. 2. 9.	£205.19. 6.	£35. 5. 0.	£31. 5. 0.	£29.14. 0.	£27. 3. 6.
200 GP	£189. 3. 8.	£54. 6. 4.	£243.10. 0.	£42.10. 0.	£37.10. 0.	£35.18. 0.	£32.15. 0.

The last SX 150 price list from November 1969 offered it for £21 less than the GP 150

Lambretta

Lambretta Concessionaires Ltd
Lambretta House Purley Way Croydon
CR9 4HD England Phone: 01 686 2499
Telex: 21138 Cables: Lambretta Croydon

TO ALL LAMBRETTA DEALERS. No. 13/69.

SX.150 SUPERSEDED BY GP.125.

It sounds strange that a 125 supersedes a 150 but the GP.125 is now in full production and is equal in performance to the current SX.150. We feel sure you will agree that it makes sense to supersede an SX.150 with the GP.125 with all the latest body styling and improved technical specification, particularly when this machine can be offered at a more economical and salient price to suit our market. £179. 19. 6d. is the figure including purchase tax - available in two colours of all white or all turquoise.

Deliveries will commence 2nd. week of December and all orders received up until 10th November for SX.150 will be fulfilled. Orders taken after that date will automatically be transferred to GP.125. Full details of profit margins are enclosed together with initial order form.

SPARE PARTS.

Please refer to your present GP spare parts catalogue which covers fully the 125 model and explains interchangeability.

5th December, 1969.

The news from December 1969 that the SX 150 was to be replaced by the GP 125, which is stated as being equal in performance when, in fact, it wasn't

20
Dealers controlled the colour choice of the Lambretta

Motor vehicles in the 1950s were rather drab in appearance, and it wasn't until the end of the decade that things began to change. More colour choice was added, but it was still somewhat limited, and nothing really stood out. The same could be said of motorcycles, all black in appearance apart from the wheels and petrol tank, even though areas to paint parts were limited. For the Lambretta, the choice was much greater because the enclosed bodywork provided a considerable area that could be painted. This meant two-tone colour options would stand out, making the machines more attractive to customers.

It was very basic in delivery, with the side panels and front horn casting offset from the rest of the bodywork. Nevertheless, it meant that there were now brighter machines in the showroom and out on the road. This paint scheme was introduced on the LD models and continued when the first Li models were introduced in 1958, these later becoming known as the series one. Even though the paint schemes took advantage of the bodywork layout, Innocenti didn't maximise it enough, or so it was felt in the UK. To take the idea forward, Lambretta Concessionaires embarked on an ambitious plan to make the colour choice not only more vibrant but unique.

The Li 150 series two had the front horn casting and side panels painted in a different colour to give a two-tone scheme

Lambretta

Newsletter

SALES & ADMINISTRATION

To: All Lambretta Dealers. No.......... 32/60.

Li.150 series II - Colour Availability.

We are now able to announce that as from today's date we can make available to all Dealers, Li.150 series II model Lambrettas finished in light grey but with side panels sprayed to your own colour choice.

This means that any Dealer wishing to have his own distinctive colour scheme, can forward a colour sample with his order and we will arrange for the machine side panels to be sprayed in a similar shade before delivery.

We believe this is the first time that an offer such as this has ever been made to the trade by either a 4-wheeled or 2-wheeled vehicle manufacturer/concessionaire, and we hope that you will take full advantage of it. The offer will remain in force until further notice.

Your orders should be forwarded for minimum quantities of five (5) machines per colour sample, together with a paint "dab", and you may rest assured that these will receive our immediate attention.

Now is the time for you to establish in your area an eye-catching and unusual colour scheme, to draw the attention of the general public to YOU, their local LAMBRETTA DEALER.

Lambretta Concessionaires Limited,
Trojan Works,
Purley Way,
Croydon, Surrey.

22nd June, 1960.

The letter sent out to dealers offering them the choice to decide on what colour option they wanted

The Li 125 came in light grey with just side panels in a different colour, and this was how the Li 150 would be offered to dealers who chose the unique paint option

In 1960, with the series two selling in its thousands, they offered dealers the choice to create their own colour combination. The option was limited to the side panels on examples where the horn casting was the same colour as the rest of the bodywork. As long as they placed a minimum order of five or more machines, the shade chosen was entirely up to them. There was a cost associated with doing this, of course, but it was minimal and the ability of dealers to offer a colour choice unique to their shop was bound to create interest. It was only offered on the Li 150, but this was the most popular model and would soon get noticed once owners rode around on the bright-looking machines.

In later years, series two Lambrettas began to appear with what looked like factory paint but not from the officially listed standard colour choice. Speculation that this couldn't be possible and that individuals repainted them seemed like the only possible explanation. The truth is it was indeed done at the factory, and while not every dealer took up the option, some did, even though there are no official documents as to the colours used.

Series two machines lined up, ready to leave the factory. Any different paint schemes the dealer requested would be done here

21
Lambretta Gran Luxe

Though the origins of the mod culture go back to the beginning of the 1960s, it wasn't until a couple of years later that it became more mainstream. Once it did, it turned into a commercial entity fuelled by the press and leading up to the mods and rockers battles of 1964. As the mod scene began to grow, scooters became the accepted mode of transport, and both Lambretta and Vespa gained approval. While some saw it as a boost to sales, those in control thought otherwise.

The management at Lambretta Concessionaires regarded the scooter-riding teenagers as bad publicity when trouble was involved and believed that it was giving the Lambretta a bad name. It must be remembered that the scooter was still regarded as a mode of transport, and that is what they wanted the public to perceive the Lambretta as. This new association with popular culture was doing more harm than good as far as they were concerned, but there seemed to be an upturn in the sale of accessories, certainly front and rear racks. The accessory side of the business had always been lucrative, and this extra boost didn't go unnoticed.

Keen to capitalise on any form of increased sales, Peter Agg instigated a variation on the Li 150 series three. This was the most popular selling machine and appealed to the younger generation because of its affordability. Realising there was a potential market, the company offered the Lambretta Gran Luxe Li 150. It was nothing unique or modified for better performance; it simply had redecorated side panels, presented in chrome instead of paint. At a cost of ten pounds more than the standard Li 150, it was only a slight increase and was quoted as "catering for the modern-day teenager".

Even though they regarded the modernist movement as a hindrance, there was no denying that all the press attention was free publicity for the Lambretta. Not attempting to capitalise on the opportunity would have been seen as a failure by the management and this was the reason why they did something about it. It was only ever going to be a short-term venture, and there was very little in the way of promotion for it; how many Gran Luxe machines actually sold remains a mystery.

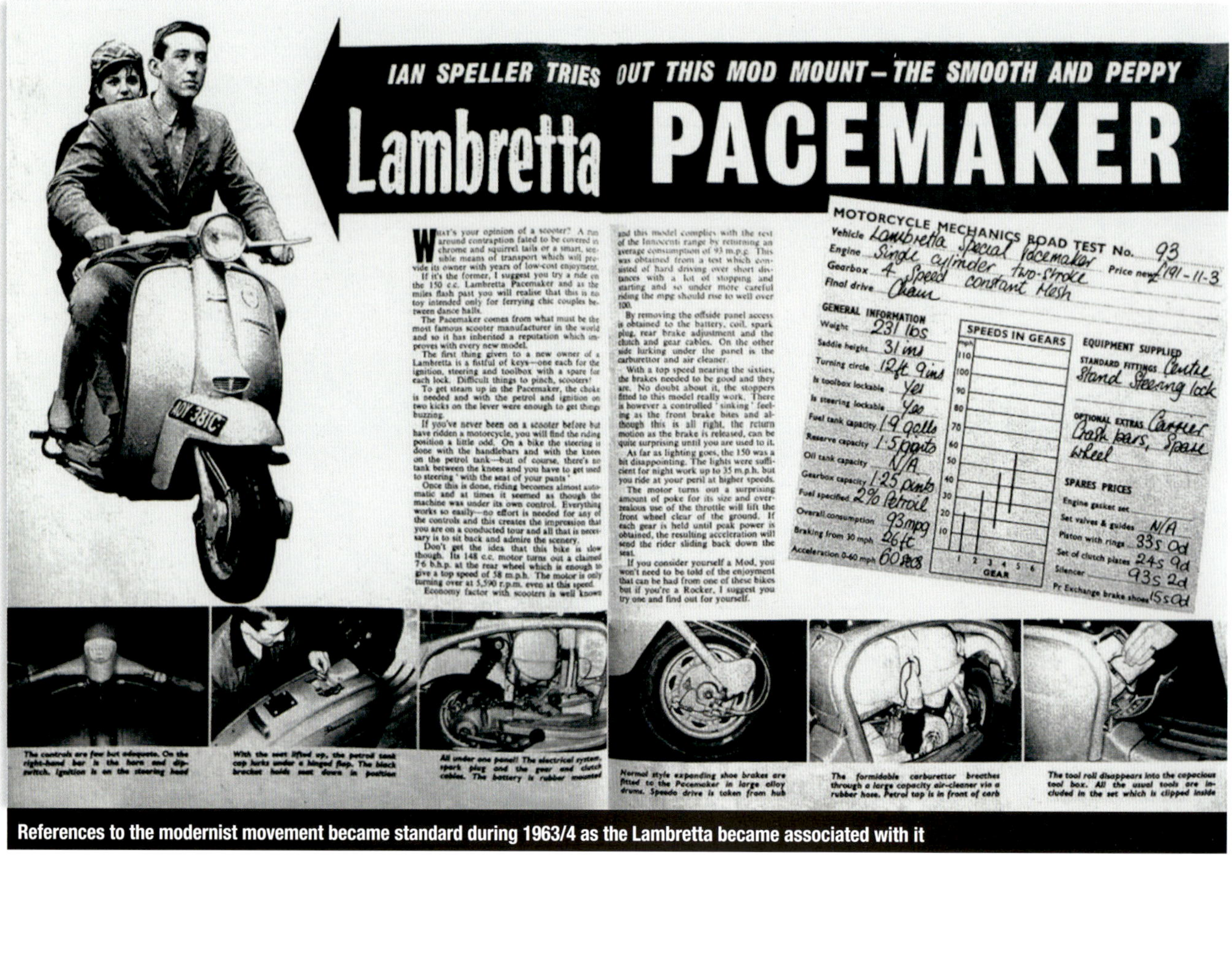

References to the modernist movement became standard during 1963/4 as the Lambretta became associated with it

MODELS

Lambretta undoubtedly have a range of machines which give little or no trouble - you don't see them back: they are indeed a very fine example of design and technical reliability. If the mass of the public cannot afford the price level of such machines, however much they may want them, the manufacturer must redesign his models to fit the purchasing power of the public. This takes time but our design team is always working for advancement on these lines. To meet the situation meantime, however, we have decided to reduce the price of the following models as from 1st October 1963, to bring them nearer the public's pocket level.

		Basic	P.T.	Price
SLIMSTYLE 150	from	£140.16.7	£29.0.11	£169.17.6
	to	£132.10.10	£27.6. 8	£159.17.6 (not inc.pillion)
SLIMSTYLE 175	from	£157.8.2.	£32.9.4.	£189.17.6.
	to	£154.1.11.	£31.15.7	£185.17.6

and to cater for the modern-day teenager by the introduction of a 150cc Slimstyle with chrome side panels to be known as the

GRAN LUXE 150	at	£140.16.7	£29.0.11.	£169.17.6

NO RETAIL PRICE LISTS OR PUBLIC ANNOUNCEMENTS WILL BE ISSUED UNTIL 1ST OCTOBER 1963 on any of these price changes.

The first mention of the Gran Luxe was in October 1963

Lambretta *Price List*

MODEL	BASIC	P/TAX	TOTAL
Cento '100'	£ 91 15 8	£18 1 10	£109 17 6
Slimstyle '125'	£112 6 9	£22 10 9	£134 17 6 PILLION EXTRA
Slimstyle '150'	£133 17 2	£26 0 4	£159 17 6 PILLION EXTRA
Slimstyle '150' Gran Luxe WITH CHROME SIDE PANELS	£142 4 7	£27 12 11	£169 17 6 INC. PILLION
Slimstyle '150' Special Pacemaker ALL GREY	£148 12 3	£28 17 9	£177 10 0 INC. DUAL SEAT
Slimstyle '150' Special Pacemaker WITH COLOURED SIDE PANELS	£150 12 1	£29 5 5	£179 17 6 INC. DUAL SEAT
G.T. 200	£167 6 11	£32 10 7	£199 17 6 INC. DUAL SEAT
Box Sidecar c/w chassis and brake	£ 57 10 0	— — —	£ 57 10 0
Sidecar chassis only c/w brake	£ 24 16 7	£ 4 13 5	£ 29 10 0

The above prices apply from March 1st. 1964 until further notice. The manufacturers reserve the right to alter prices and specifications without prior notice.

The only listing for it, including price, dated March 1964 and disappearing soon afterwards

22
The sale of Lambretta aftermarket accessories was a sackable offence

Becoming an authorised Lambretta dealer was a lucrative proposition in the UK. As the Lambretta gained a more significant market share, more dealers wanted to become involved in selling it. Once approved, it was almost like a licence to print money, making a profit from selling the machines and the aftersales side that came with it. This included servicing and selling accessories, which was regarded

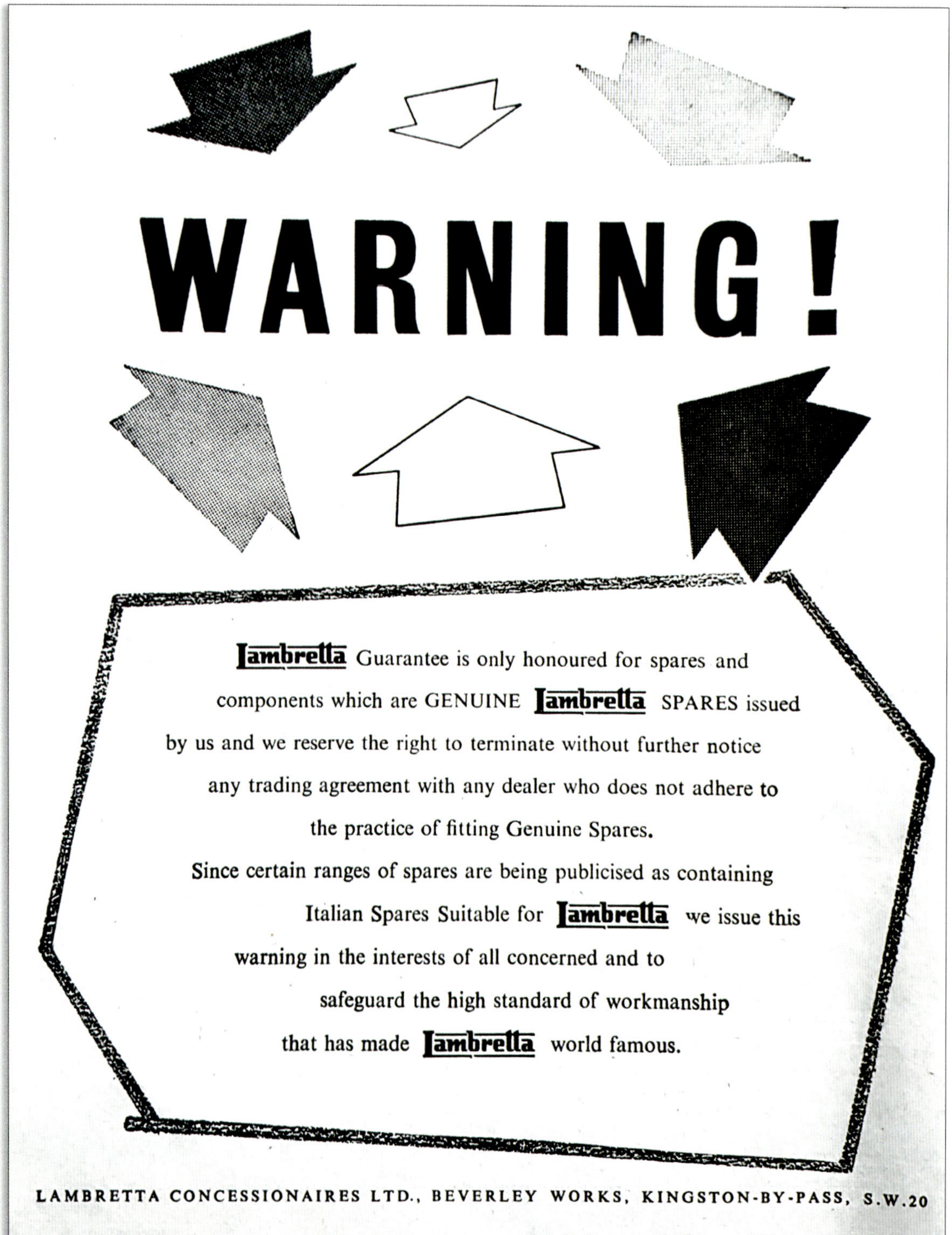

As far back as the mid-1950s, Lambretta Concessionaires warned dealers of the consequences of selling non-genuine spares. So much so that they placed this advert in magazines to remind them of the warning

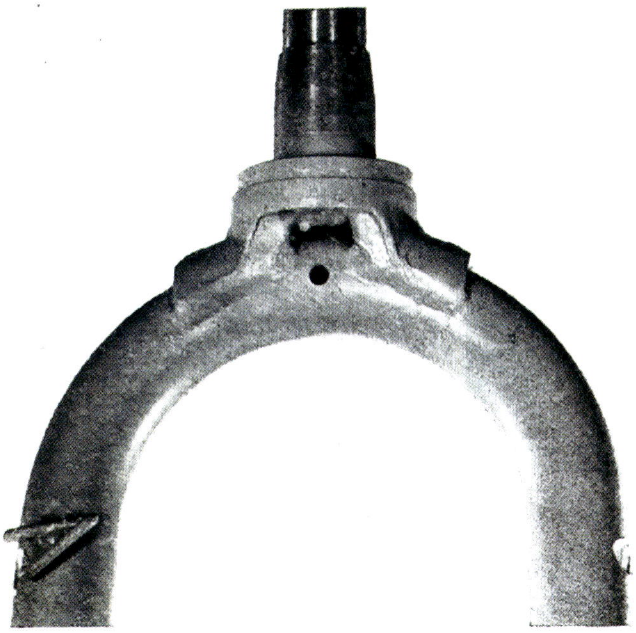

The Lambretta Page

Is it wrong to buy non-genuine spare parts for Lambretta and other scooters?

We say—most definitely—it is wrong; that it is false economy and can lead to serious accidents.

That is why we are using this space to discuss a question over which it is all too easy to be "penny wise and pound foolish."

Take a look at these two pictures. They show two front forks. Above you see a genuine Lambretta replacement. Below, a non-genuine part.

Superficially, they look very much alike. Examine them a little more closely and you will see some vital differences.

The stem of the non-genuine fork is not tapered. It lacks the in-built strength of the genuine Lambretta product. Some non-genuine forks are actually machine-tapered to make them look—and feel!—like the genuine article.

Now look at the boss. In the case of the authentic part it is welded. The other is merely brazed. The fork above has arms made of a continuous horse-shoe tube, with great inherent strength. In the other the two arms are made of separate tubes, brazed at the boss.

The genuine fork weighs 10 lbs., the other only 8¾ lbs. As far as strength is concerned there is really no comparison. It is a good example of what we mean when we say it can be potentially dangerous to use non-genuine spare parts.

Because they are usually cheaper, some short-sighted scooter owners buy non-genuine parts without giving a thought to the fact that they are made from inferior materials. They allow these sub-standard parts to be fitted to machines built to very high standards of quality control and which can easily be expensively damaged by the failure of defective "pattern" parts.

We came across a clear-cut example of this only the other day. A Lambretta owner who saved 17s 6d. by buying a non-genuine crankshaft found himself saddled with a bill for £40 when the crankshaft failed and wrecked his engine.

Not that you always save money, even initially, by buying non-genuine parts. What you pay for them varies greatly and depends on where you buy them. Some non-genuine parts are even sold at the same price as genuine Lambretta parts.

Some traders are content with a smaller profit and sometimes offer quite a big saving. The fact is, you never know where you stand with these non-genuine parts. The traders handling them charge as much as they can get away with. And the scooter owners patronising them get none of the protection and guarantee afforded by accredited Lambretta dealers.

When they have their machines repaired Lambretta owners should make quite sure that genuine Innocenti parts have been used. It is a wise precaution to look for the Innocenti mark, though even that is sometimes fraudulently copied.

It will be possible soon to identify genuine Lambretta parts positively by means of an attached official lead seal. Better still, make sure of getting genuine parts by going only to official appointed Lambretta dealers and service agents who handle only the genuine article.

Some non-genuine parts are manufactured in England, but most are imported. Remember this: in the event of an accident, injury caused by the failure of a non-genuine part, insurance claims are liable to be rejected out of hand.

Special care should be taken when buying parts like crown wheels and pinions, clutch plates, shock absorbers, front axles, forks and silencers.

If ever you are in any doubt, do not hesitate to get in touch with Mr. E. Rosso, our Spare Parts Purchasing Manager.

Please believe us when we say that in this matter of non-genuine parts we are not so much concerned by the possibility of losing your custom as with your personal safety and with Lambretta's high reputation for reliability, which can so easily be tarnished by the failure of non-genuine, sub-standard parts.

The problem was discussed thoroughly in the press about the dangers of using aftermarket spares

Don Noys' first scooter business as he began to make a name for himself in the industry

Don, during one of his record-breaking runs on his well-known and modified and tuned Lambretta GT 200

Having successfully established several British speed records, Lambretta Concessionaires took out an advert to maximise his achievements. A few months later their relationship broke down as Don was stripped of his dealership

as the way to make the most profit when becoming an authorised dealer.

It wasn't uncommon for even a small shop to sell 50 machines monthly, which meant the customer base would grow considerably each year. Another advantage a dealer had was the form of protection of their investment due to how far apart dealers were located. In a small town, there may only be one or two at most, with them separated by several miles. This meant there was no chance of saturating the market by having too many shops close to each other fighting for business. In big cities like London and Birmingham, there were obviously more, but they were still separated far enough apart that each shop had an extensive catchment area.

Becoming a dealer wasn't just a case of owning a shop. It came with a strict set of rules outlined in the contract when signing up. This meant such things as loyalty to the brand and not selling other makes of scooter which was standard in the industry. It also required significant investment in a workshop with all the correct factory tools and qualified staff for servicing and repairs. The other major requirement was to carry spares and stock for each model, and this was where problems began to arise. Some dealers argued that carrying too much stock

Now a free agent, he brought the Ancillotti brothers over to the UK to break records on their Lambretta. He was instrumental in setting up the Ancillotti range of tuning items with Nannucci, which became a huge success

was unnecessary, and when a new model was introduced, they might get stuck with soon-to-be-obsolete parts.

With the factory having such vast stockpiles of spares, dealers thought it was easier if they ordered what was required when necessary rather than carry the stock in their shop. It was part of the agreement that a certain amount had to be taken by a dealer, so in effect, Lambretta Concessionaires were selling a lot of components they didn't require. With the Lambretta being so successful, it didn't take long for aftermarket parts and accessories to flood the market, and dealers were tempted to buy them. One of the main reasons was that they were much cheaper than genuine spares, so potentially, there was more profit to be made. The main issue with aftermarket spares is there was no quality control and some items may not be fit for purpose. This could be dangerous if a substandard component failed and meant the rider was at risk.

Lambretta Concessionaires stipulated in the dealer contract that if they used non-factory items this would put them in breach of the terms and result in the dealership being taken away. While the danger of fitting non-factory mechanical parts was potentially very real, the same could not be said for cosmetic items, such as racks, for example. A dealer buying these elsewhere wasn't putting anyone at risk – they were just eating into Lambretta Concessionaires' profits. Consequently, some dealers were unhappy that the company was making more money out of them than they should. The customer also felt the knock-on effect because if an aftermarket part was fitted and failed, it wouldn't be covered under the warranty.

The whole process of spares was constantly monitored, and letters were regularly sent out to dealers regarding the punishment they would face should they decide to carry this practice out. The question was, would the company stand by its rules and sack anyone flouting them, taking their dealership away? The answer was yes, they would, and the most high-profile case came about in the mid-1960s.

Don Noys was a London-based dealer who had been selling Lambrettas for a long time. Initially starting with the Shead Scooter Co. in Tulse Hill before moving on to Don Noys Limited in Crown Dale. Don had become something of a celebrity in his own right, often featured in magazines and for modifying the Lambretta. In 1964/5, he attempted several speed records on a modified GT 200, setting national records in the process.

His achievements gained great publicity for the Lambretta in the national and motorcycle press, with Lambretta Concessionaires even using his exploits in advertising. However, Don was using some aftermarket companies for Lambretta items, and Lambretta Concessionaires became wary of this fact. On several occasions, he was warned that his Lambretta dealership would be taken away from him if he didn't stop. Heedless of the warnings, he continued. The main problem was his association with Nannucci, who had a huge catalogue of Lambretta-related items. Lambretta Concessionaires saw them as their arch nemesis, taking huge revenue away from the company. After a final warning was ignored, Don Noys had his Lambretta dealership taken away, and it was a stark warning of what the consequences would be for anyone wishing to go down this path.

Don continued to sell aftermarket Lambretta spares and, by this time, had a Honda dealership, so his business continued. In an act of defiance against those who had sacked him, he was instrumental in bringing the Ancillotti brothers over to the UK to attempt speed records on their modified Lambretta. Another part of this was to set up the Ancillotti brand of Lambretta-related tuning products, such as exhausts, cylinders and seats. The company chosen to take it on was none other than Nannucci, and it was his way of giving a two-fingered salute to those who had stripped him of his Lambretta dealership.

23
How secretive was the news of the Lambretta finishing production?

It is common knowledge that Lambretta production finished in May 1971, but how much of a secret was it? Innocenti as a company was in deep financial trouble by 1970, and while some of it was due to mismanagement, there is no doubt that the previous year's industrial strikes were also to blame. What was known as the 'Hot Autumn' was a culmination of unions joining together to get better conditions and pay for workers. With all major companies being affected, Innocenti was also drawn into the dispute. The scooter production line came to a halt, but so did the other sections of the company, which made up the majority of the workforce and, therefore, put even more strain on the financial side.

British Leyland was already planning on being more involved in the company because Innocenti had been producing their cars under licence. This agreement went back to 1959 when the company was known as the British Motor Corporation (BMC), and by 1970, almost a million cars had been produced at the Milan factory. Negotiations about British Leyland giving the ailing company a cash injection were known, but it surprised everyone when they bought the company outright. This was so they could open up a European car plant with the idea of producing millions of cars to sell on the continent without having to export them from the UK.

This finally happened in May 1971, and it is alleged the very first decision was to halt the production of the Lambretta. The fallout from it was immense, and while it was devastating news in Italy, it didn't go down much better in the UK. Everyone at Lambretta Concessionaires presumed Peter Agg was well aware of what was happening and, being head of the company, would have been kept up to date with the negotiations. This wasn't true, and he knew nothing about the decision and vowed to try and do something about it.

In later years, he explained that losing the product his company relied on without prior knowledge came as a great shock. He also admitted to feeling guilty about it because he had negotiated the Innocenti/BMC deal in 1959 and therefore felt, in a way, that he was responsible for it happening. No one could have seen what was coming all those years before, and no one blamed him for the decision being made.

When it happened, he tried to find a solution, not only asking for the decision to be reconsidered but the possibility of the production line being moved to the UK. That would have been impossible and was proven by how long it took for that to happen. The Grand Prix production line was sold to Scooters India Limited (SIL), and moving the equipment and setting it up over there was a huge undertaking – with it being more than five years before it was up and running and the first machines were built. With Peter Agg taking over Suzuki GB in 1969, he had that to focus on and therefore concentrated on building that side of the business up, cushioning the blow. Had he not taken the Suzuki option, he may have put up a bigger fight to save the Lambretta, but reversing British Leyland's decision would never happen.

To prove that what he said in later years about the whole affair was true, two press releases surfaced, which are the last ones known to have been written before the decision was made. One dated March 26, 1971 and the other in May, just before the announcement, and to explain new stock arriving from the Innocenti factory in Milan sometime in July. Also mentioned is how well the Lambretta was selling, the upturn in trade in the first few months of the year, and that the outlook was good. These letters show that even Peter Agg knew nothing about the impending decision and what a well-kept secret it was.

Lambretta

Lambretta Concessionaires Ltd
Lambretta House Purley Way Croydon
CR9 4HD England Phone: 01 686 2499
Telex: 21138 Cables: Lambretta Croydon

TO ALL LAMBRETTA DEALERS No. 5/71.

GP.200 AVAILABILITY.

The first three months of 1971 have exceeded all expectations and dealers up and down the country have been telling us that the scooter market has, once again, become really alive. We thank all our dealers sincerely for their active support in bringing this about.

However, this situation is not without its problems because, obviously, when our sales programme was made many months ago we must confess that we did not, at that time, foresee the possibility of the surge which has taken place. As a result, our supplies of GP.200 are now exhausted until July so far as new orders are concerned. We have, however, managed to obtain from the Italian production line a quantity of GP.200 Electronics without battery lighting. We feel that these will help us to bridge the gap until new supplies arrive in July. This model will come in at the special price structure indicated by the enclosed chart.

Supplies of this model will be available mid May and will come in Red and Ochre only.

We apologise for the inconvenience which we know this will cause but further quantities of the GP.200 Electronic will be available. In giving you this information we would advise you that the electronic model has proved so successful that further supplies will all be to this specification and no further supplies of the standard model will be available. All orders at present in hand will be transferred to this model (GP.200 Electronic with battery lighting) unless dealers indicate otherwise.

Dealers wishing to make sure of models from the special delivery referred to above should complete and return to us the enclosed order form as quickly as possible.

26th March, 1971.

The press release dated March 26, 1971 is a few weeks before Lambretta production finished at the Innocenti factory in Milan. Full of optimism, it predicts a successful year for sales, but sadly, that would never happen

Lambretta

Lambretta Concessionaires Ltd
Lambretta House Purley Way Croydon
CR9 4HD England Phone: 01 686 2499
Telex: 21138 Cables: Lambretta Croydon

TO ALL LAMBRETTA DEALERS. No. 7/71.

LAMBRETTA DELIVERIES.

Everyone must be aware of the current scooter and motor cycle boom. Our sales forecasts have been far exceeded and our production capacity for some models is already exhausted.

The problems of strike, wage claims and other industrial difficulties, as well as the increased lead times for raw materials, lead us to inform you that the delivery position obtains as follows :-

GP.200 - no more orders can be accepted until after the factory holiday shut-down in August.

Spanish LI.150 - no more orders for delivery before July. However, limited supplies will be available from July onwards. It is necessary to increase immediately the recommended retail price. This includes orders at present outstanding.

The new recommended retail price will be as follows :-

£142.93 plus £42.04 purchase tax = £184.97
Main Dealer margin C.O.D. Terms = £29. 40

GP.150 - Delays may occur on specific colour ranges but stock available.
GP.125

VEGA - all available ex-stock.
COMETA - Limited supplies only. Colours Apple Green & Ochre.

We give this information to our Dealers so that they are fully in the picture in regard to the production and supply problems which are at present prevailing.

May, 1971.

This press release is dated May 1971, just days before the decision was made, mentioning the industrial action in Italy being responsible for delays. It states that the GP 200 will not be available until August at the earliest

24
Who invented the dual control Lambretta?

The dual control Lambretta was a UK invention introduced by Lambretta Concessionaires in 1960. The idea was for an instructor to sit in the pillion passenger position and teach beginners the techniques of how to ride a Lambretta. Initially, it was based on modifying a Li 150 series two model. The instructor would operate a set of fixed handlebars, which were positioned between the two seats, allowing him to override the brakes and switch off the engine through a cutout button. This is similar to how a learner car would be operated, even though it meant an awkward riding position for the instructor.

The concept was thought up by Mallaby & Co, an official Lambretta dealer based in Yorkshire, and put forward to Peter Agg. The notion appealed to him due to the negative press about scooters and motorbikes being dangerous and responsible for many deaths and injuries on UK roads. Such a machine, where an instructor could properly teach learner riders, seemed like the perfect way to show that road safety was being taken seriously. A prototype was built at the Croydon factory and demonstrated to the Department of Transport to get backing for the idea.

On October 27, 1960, the new dual-control Lambretta was launched in the presence of Lord Chesham, the Parliamentary Secretary to the Minister of Transport and the assembled press. Coverage was promising, with no negative comments, and it was seen as a positive step in road safety. The problem was finding someone who would buy it – because it was only of use to driving schools and dealers who would teach potentially new customers. Therefore, it had a limited market. Very few dealers took the option up, with many regarding it as a cheap publicity campaign by Lambretta Concessionaires trying to gain press coverage by being concerned over rider safety. How many were sold is unknown, but with poor sales the idea was abandoned a few months later. When the first demonstrations took place, in a strange twist, the photographer used for the publicity shots was the inventor's son.

Lambretta

request the pleasure of the company of

at 12 noon on Thursday, 27th October 1960 at

the Waldorf Hotel, W.C.2

on the occasion of the introduction, in the presence of

The Rt. Hon. Lord Chesham, Parliamentary Secretary,

Ministry of Transport.

of the Dual Control Lambretta Tuition Scooter.

R.S.V.P.
Lambretta,
Public Relations,
Trojan Works,
Purley Way, Croydon, Surrey.

Snack Buffet.

The press launch was by invitation only

Lambretta

Newsletter

SALES & ADMINISTRATION

To: All Lambretta Dealers. No......... 63/60.

DUAL CONTROL LAMBRETTA.

We are pleased to be able to inform you that on Thursday, 27th October, Lambretta Concessionaires Limited will formally introduce the new dual control Lambretta scooter.

We regret the delay which has occurred in the making of this announcement, brought about by difficulty in establishing a date on which this could be arranged with the Ministry of Transport, but we are glad to be able to advise you that this scheme is now going ahead with their full backing, and Lord Chesham, the Parliamentary Secretary to the Minister of Transport, will be attending the launching ceremony, along with many leading personalities from the National and Trade press, and Road Safety Organisations.

Most Dealers will by now have received their dual control machines, and now is the time for you to arrange advertising and publicity in your local press so as to join with us in the first positive step forward in combating the adverse publicity which two-wheeled vehicles have suffered during the past six months in connection with road accident figures.

We shall be circulating within the course of the next few days, details of the advertising blocks which we shall have available on the dual control Lambretta and, as stated in our newsletter No. 60/60, we feel sure that the close co-ordination of our combined advertising, concentrated on the 27th/28th of this month, will gain for us all, the maximum benefit.

17th October, 1960.

Lambretta Concessionaires Limited,
Trojan Works,
Purley Way, Croydon, Surrey.

One of several press releases regarding the launch of the dual-control Lambretta in 1962

A rather nervous-looking learner rider awaits a lesson in controlling the Lambretta in this press shot

Another publicity photograph showing the awkward position the instructor had to sit in due to lack of space for the handlebars

This photo from the dispatch area of the factory made it look like many dual-control Lambrettas were being ordered when, in fact, sales were very poor

25
Filtrate Lambretta racer

One of the biggest myths and legends is the Filtrate Lambretta racer story. Over the years, it has been subject to constant speculation, which has exaggerated what happened so much that getting a clear understanding of it is almost impossible. There are so many aspects to what went on that breaking it down into different sections is the only way to give a decent explanation. Even then, some parts remain a mystery, but after extensive research for *Scootering* magazine, and this publication, it is now possible to make better sense of it.

One of the most popular misconceptions is that it originated with Lambretta Concessionaires, which is wrong. The idea came from Ernie Hall, who was renowned for building racing motorcycles. Ernie worked for Filtrate Oils, based in Leeds, and along with co-worker Robert Forrest-Webb, embarked on the creation of a racing Lambretta. The intent was to establish a world record over certain disciplines with top speed as the main goal. In the early 1950s, Innocenti achieved 125mph on the Siluro 125 Lambretta, even though it scarcely resembled the original machine with its fully aerodynamic bodywork. In the UK, interest had been revived in breaking that speed record with the Hills-Healy record attempt and the exploits of Don Noys on his modified TV/GT 200.

Ernie realised that achieving it would require a heavily modified machine in terms of both the engine and streamlining. It was decided that an existing TV/GT 200 would be used for the project's base, and that is when Lambretta Concessionaires became involved. They had already done work with Filtrate using their two-stroke oil during one of several 24 hours from London to Milan attempts. This time it was reversed, because Ernie contacted them about supplying the machine. Peter Agg, realising the huge marketing potential of the project, duly agreed to provide a TV 200 for it, which was their only involvement regarding the machine itself.

The Lambretta Concessionaires/Filtrate connection went back a long way, and in 1965, they had collaborated on a London to Milan in 24-hours record attempt

Marlene Parker sitting astride the machine at a press conference at the Royal Garden Hotel in Kensington. The fuel injector is clearly visible

Marlene on board the machine at Monza in December 1965 during the record attempt

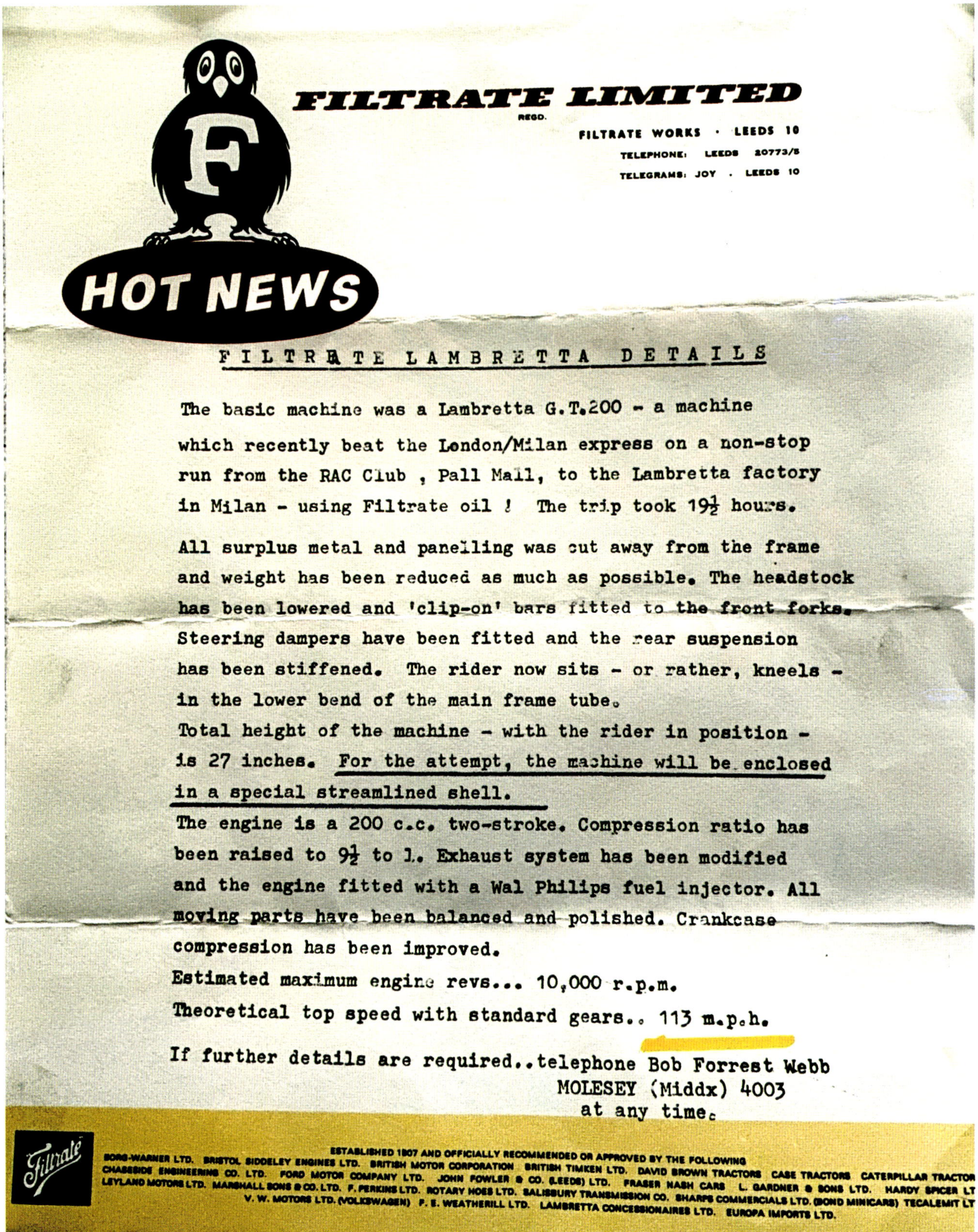

FILTRATE LIMITED
REGD.
FILTRATE WORKS · LEEDS 10
TELEPHONE: LEEDS 20773/5
TELEGRAMS: JOY · LEEDS 10

HOT NEWS

FILTRATE LAMBRETTA DETAILS

The basic machine was a Lambretta G.T.200 - a machine which recently beat the London/Milan express on a non-stop run from the RAC Club , Pall Mall, to the Lambretta factory in Milan - using Filtrate oil ! The trip took 19½ hours.

All surplus metal and panelling was cut away from the frame and weight has been reduced as much as possible. The headstock has been lowered and 'clip-on' bars fitted to the front forks. Steering dampers have been fitted and the rear suspension has been stiffened. The rider now sits - or rather, kneels - in the lower bend of the main frame tube.
Total height of the machine - with the rider in position - is 27 inches. For the attempt, the machine will be enclosed in a special streamlined shell.
The engine is a 200 c.c. two-stroke. Compression ratio has been raised to 9½ to 1. Exhaust system has been modified and the engine fitted with a Wal Philips fuel injector. All moving parts have been balanced and polished. Crankcase compression has been improved.
Estimated maximum engine revs... 10,000 r.p.m.
Theoretical top speed with standard gears.. 113 m.p.h.

If further details are required..telephone Bob Forrest Webb
MOLESEY (Middx) 4003
at any time.

Filtrate
ESTABLISHED 1907 AND OFFICIALLY RECOMMENDED OR APPROVED BY THE FOLLOWING
BORG-WARNER LTD. BRISTOL SIDDELEY ENGINES LTD. BRITISH MOTOR CORPORATION BRITISH TIMKEN LTD. DAVID BROWN TRACTORS CASE TRACTORS CATERPILLAR TRACTOR
CHASESIDE ENGINEERING CO. LTD. FORD MOTOR COMPANY LTD. JOHN FOWLER & CO. (LEEDS) LTD. FRASER NASH CARS L. GARDNER & SONS LTD. HARDY SPICER LT
LEYLAND MOTORS LTD. MARSHALL SONS & CO. LTD. F. PERKINS LTD. ROTARY HOES LTD. SALISBURY TRANSMISSION CO. SHARPS COMMERCIALS LTD. (BOND MINICARS) TECALEMIT LT
V. W. MOTORS LTD. (VOLKSWAGEN) F. E. WEATHERILL LTD. LAMBRETTA CONCESSIONAIRES LTD. EUROPA IMPORTS LTD.

The press release from Filtrate for their racer mentions fitting a Wal Phillips fuel injector to the engine. It also mentions a possible top speed of 113mph which is where some of the exaggerated speeds it supposedly set might have come from

The full Lambretta was stripped down to its frame tube, which the rider would lay prone on, with the steering controlled on the forks. The engine was bored out to a capacity of 225cc and fitted with a Wal Phillips fuel injector. This was later changed to an Amal MK 1, which was thought to be on the engine initially, but at the time the bike was built, they hadn't been invented – so that couldn't have been possible. A side draft Dellorto carburettor was also fitted and features in some of the images taken, but this was after the initial attempt was made and it was used later in testing.

The fairing was made by Ernie himself and was made from aluminium moulded into shape. It was a two-piece item with a fairing at the front to cut through the air

Once back in the UK, the machine was taken to a sprint meeting held by the NSA, again with Marlene on it. Here held on the start line by the chock and block system, the Dellorto carburettor was now fitted and is visible

MEN ONLY SAYS A.C.U.;

The A.C.U. last week clamped down on plans by Filtrate and Lambretta for a "World Scooter Speed Record" bid at Monza Italy on Decembere the second by a girl.

The union after talks with the F.I.M. told the backers that an international licence-necessary for a record bid-could not be issued to a woman.

However, Filtrate Spokesman Bob Webb said last week that they still intend to attack the so-called record, but with a male rider.

A brief quote from Robert Forrest-Webb about returning to Monza in 1966 and this time with a male rider, even though it was never mentioned who that would be

WHITE LEATHER SCOOTER SPEED GIRL GETS
RACING CAR TEST AT BRANDS

Petite, 22-year old Bristol taxi driver, Marlene Parker, realised the first stage of her ambition to be a world champion racing driver, when she underwent a test at Brands Hatch Racing Stables in a single seater.

Marlene, who in February, signed a contract with the Lambretta-Trojan Group to drive both two and four wheel vehicles, is shortly to make another attempt to break world speed records on the Lambretta „Jet" scooter which has a potential top speed of 125 m.p.h.

Said Racing Stables` instructor, Syd Fox: „Marlene got a B-Plus which is above average, even for men. She`s got technical ability and, although cautions, wanted to go faster all the time."

Said Marlene: „On the scooter I`m lying on my tummy – in the single seater it``s like lying in the bath. I bet it gets pretty hot, too, sometimes!"

If Marlene completes the instruction course successfully, she will begin her motor racing career by driving the 2-litre Elva_BMW sports racing car, manufactured by Elva Cars at Rys, the Racing Car Division of the Lambretta-Trojan Group.

Pictures Shows: Marlene Parker being given a final briefing for her first solo in a single seater by Mr. Geoff. Clark who heads the Brands Hatch Racing Stables.
In the foreground is the Lambretta „Jet" scooter, developed by Mr. Bob Webb, on which she is soon to attempt new world speed records.

May 13, 1966

P. Garnett Keeler

Public Relations Officer,
Lambretta-Trojan Group,
Purley Way, Croydon, Surrey

A press release regarding Marlene once she was signed up by the Trojan group, outlining her ambitions to go racing. A quote of 125mph for the Filtrate racer, now referred to as the Lambretta Jet, is mentioned again, creating more speculation and exaggeration of what speed it reached

The photograph taken of Marlene for the press release as they attempted to mould her into a racing driver

The machine on display in Mike Karslake's museum in the 1980s

and one at the back to allow it to run off the machine more smoothly. It was mounted to the frame by steel struts bolted to the fairing. Once complete, the idea was to test it before going to Monza to make the attempt and iron out any potential problems. They believed that the engine, at maximum revs of 10,000rpm, could reach a potential speed of 113mph.

The most significant talking point over the whole affair was the rider. Ernie thought that a woman would be naturally lighter than a man, and a reduction in weight would benefit any racing machine. This had helped to attract Lambretta Concessionaires to the project, because the idea of a woman rider would gain further publicity beyond that generated by the record attempt itself. Specifically, women were not allowed to attempt world speed records as outlined by the FIM, which was the governing body. Announcing that a woman was to challenge this discriminatory policy would spark huge controversy and press coverage, which they wanted. All of this would bring free attention, costing the company nothing, and with the *Daily Express* taking an interest, that is precisely what happened.

A competition was set up for women to apply to be the chosen rider, and there were a total of 67 applicants. That number was slowly whittled down via a series of high-profile selections to gain maximum exposure. Bob

The front cover from *Practical Scooter* November 1966, which shows it with the small motorcycle fairing fitted to it once back in the UK

It now resides on permanent display as Scooter Center Cologne, fully preserved

The original fairings were thought lost forever but resurfaced and were photographed in 2024, awaiting preservation

Wilkinson ran the Lambretta Club Great Britain for Lambretta Concessionaires and was the advertising manager in charge of the whole affair. Christine Jackson, Pat Cowburn and Marlene Parker were the final three women chosen. According to press reports, the decision was made by drawing lots, which Marlene won. Christine Jackson was the preferred choice because she was already a gifted Lambretta rider and would have been more suited, but the decision was final and that was how it stayed.

The scheduled record attempt meeting was set for December 1965, with a test to take place at Snetterton in November, but that was cancelled due to snow and ice on the track, making it impossible to run. This meant an acute lack of preparation before going to Italy. However, on December 2, 1965, at Monza, with certified officials there to record the speed, Marlene made her attempt. Reports said the engine had starting issues and constantly misfired, which had been a problem on the only previous engine fire-up. Several runs were made, with one resulting in a high-speed seizure, almost throwing Marlene from the machine. It was deemed too dangerous to attempt any more runs, so the day was cancelled and considered a failure. Marlene got close to breaking Don Noys' quarter-mile record on one of the runs and reached a top speed of just over 80mph, but it was way under what had been predicted.

Press reports at the time claimed a speed of over 110mph was reached and later over 125mph, but none of these claims were ever proven or backed up. The rumours must be regarded as pure speculation unless evidence to prove otherwise ever comes to light. After the failed attempt, the team announced they would return to Monza in April 1966 with the machine thoroughly tested and any issues resolved. Robert Forrest Webb was even quoted as saying that a male rider would be used to make it official.

Before that could happen, the Filtrate Lambretta was taken to a sprint meeting in the UK, and Marlene once again rode it. Don Noys was also present, and Christine Jackson was invited to try his record-breaking machine. Not only did she break a record on the day, but she went quicker than the Filtrate racer, which was still plagued by misfires, giving her great satisfaction in the knowledge that she was on the superior machine. The trip back to Monza never happened, and this is where the story ended, or so you might think. In reality, there remained a number of loose ends.

Marlene had become a celebrity in her own right thanks to the press coverage and, keen to capitalise on her new status, she was offered a contract by Lambretta Concessionaires and the Trojan group. Ideally she would have become an international racer, and she briefly competed on a 500cc Triumph sprinter belonging to Phil Manzano from the National Sprint Association. She did this at several meetings with the idea of switching to four wheels and racing an Elva sports car built by Trojan. None of this materialised, and Marlene disappeared from the racing scene altogether before moving to Australia.

What about the machine itself, which was returned to Lambretta Concessionaires when it came back to the UK? That was sold to Arthur Francis in Watford, who campaigned it at a few sprint events, and this was when it was named Atlanta V. After a while, he stopped using it. When Mike Karslake opened his Lambretta museum in the 1980s, Arthur donated the machine to him. It stayed there until the museum closed after Mike's passing and was then sold along with all the other exhibits when they were auctioned off. It ended up in Germany and now resides on permanent display at Scooter Center in Cologne, having been preserved, but there is one final twist to the story.

When Arthur Francis received the machine in 1966, the fairings were missing so he fitted a small motorcycle front fairing to it. This was photographed for an article in *Practical Scooter* in 1966 and it is still fitted to it. In later years, when in Mike Karslake's possession, he was asked what happened to the original fairings and he explained that Arthur Francis didn't get them with the machine. He was told they had been scrapped because they were too cumbersome to transport, and that's the way the story remained. That is, until a motorcycle journalist visited Ernie Hall in 2021 to interview him and look at his old collection of racing motorcycles.

There were several hundred stockpiled over the years, scattered in outbuildings, and in amongst them, lo and behold, were the missing fairings from the Filtrate racer. Ernie explained that he was a bit annoyed at the time for not getting much credit for his creation, with all the attention focused on the woman riding it. When the machine was bought back from Monza, he took the fairings back because they were his property, not forgetting how long it had taken to craft them. They had lain there in his shed ever since and had remarkably survived in good condition. Sadly, Ernie passed away a few months later, and his entire collection went to auction, including the fairings. A private bidder bought them and they are now in safe hands – ensuring their preservation for the future.

Along with the fairings was a small amount of paperwork which revealed the work done to the machine and the expected top speed. The unfortunate lack of testing meant the project was doomed to failure from the outset, and it may be the reason for not returning to Monza a few months later, even though the no official reason why was ever disclosed. While some aspects of the project remain a mystery, many of the myths surrounding it can now be laid to rest.

26
The improved disc brake

Innocenti stunned the world when they launched the TV 175 series three in 1962. While the sleek lines of the Slimstyle gave the Lambretta a modern look, it was the disc brake that grabbed the attention. It was the first production two-wheeled vehicle in the world to have one fitted, making the Lambretta unique. The cable-operated single-pot calliper may have been basic, but the improved stopping power was welcome. Once the 200cc Lambretta arrived in the shape of the TV 200, that and all other 200cc models would have one fitted.

Italian bicycle manufacturer Campagnolo produced it for Innocenti, and getting it to fit in the hub diameter for a 10in wheel was a design master class. However, it wasn't without its problems, mainly due to the amount of pressure the cable-operated calliper could exert on the disc. This was helped somewhat by using a thicker inner cable, but the other problem was that the calliper was held in place by a circlip. This was a potential weak point as more pressure was applied, and it was also exposed directly to the elements.

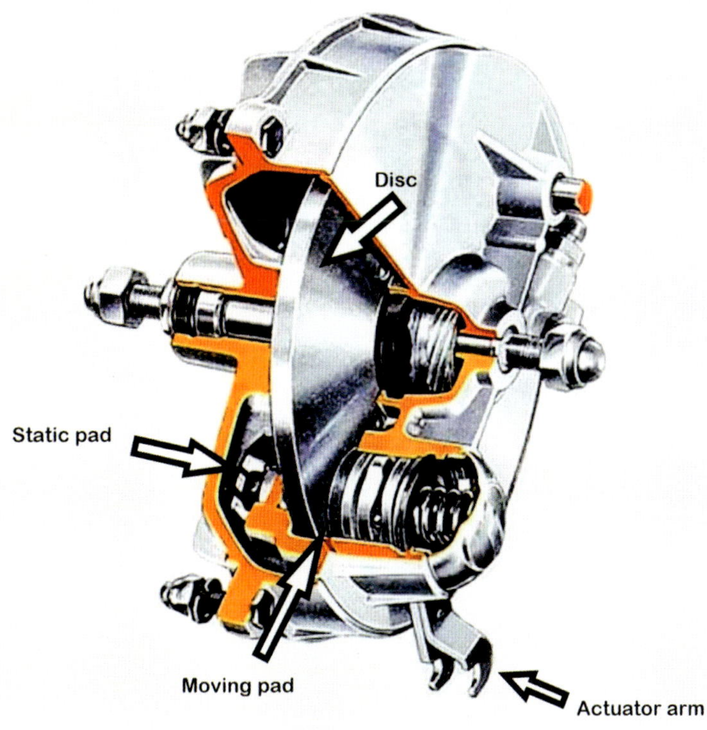

The original disc brake design was first introduced on the TV 175 in 1962 and used until production of the Lambretta finished in 1971

It was made by Italian bicycle manufacturer Campagnolo

PEPPING UP THAT DISC BRAKE

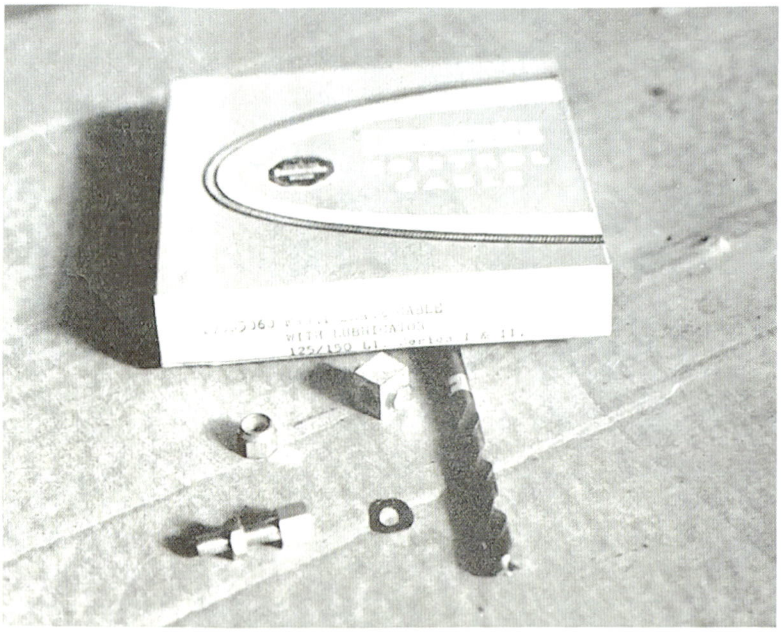

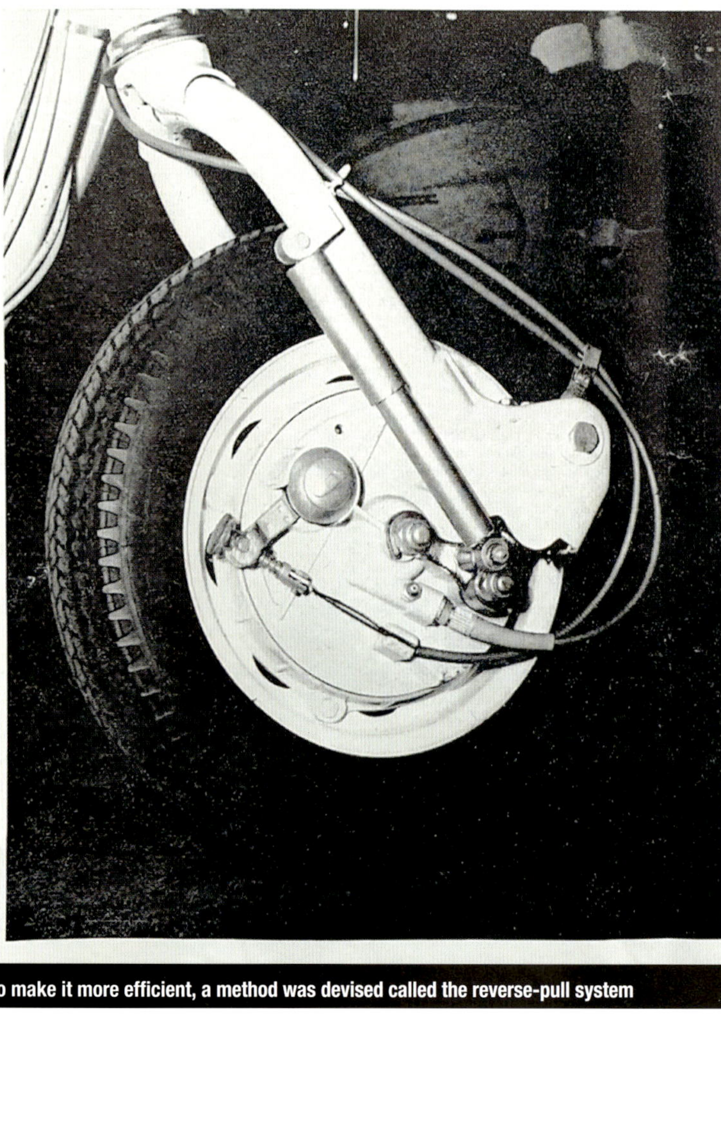

The disc brake on the Lambretta GT.200 and the later TV.175 models has not given complete satisfaction. Complaints were on two points;

1 Too much hand pressure was needed to apply the disc brake. Nothing happened unless you grabbed it hard.

2 The disc brake was sometimes noisy and tended to come on with a jerk.

In our April 1967 issue we gave detailed instructions covering both points. We described how you could switch the brake cable so that the disc brake came on full chat with the lightest of touches at the brake lever—you could put the brake on hard with one finger. The new arrangement is shown in our photograph on the left. The cost of the job is about ten shillings. You can do it yourself, and our photograph up above shows you all the bits and pieces you need.

In the same April 1967 issue we also gave full instructions for adjusting the brake and explained how it was that the disc could sometimes stick. As to the noise, think nothing of it. If the disc brake on your Lambretta does NOT rattle a bit you should have it adjusted. You can do the job yourself without difficulty.

To make it more efficient, a method was devised called the reverse-pull system

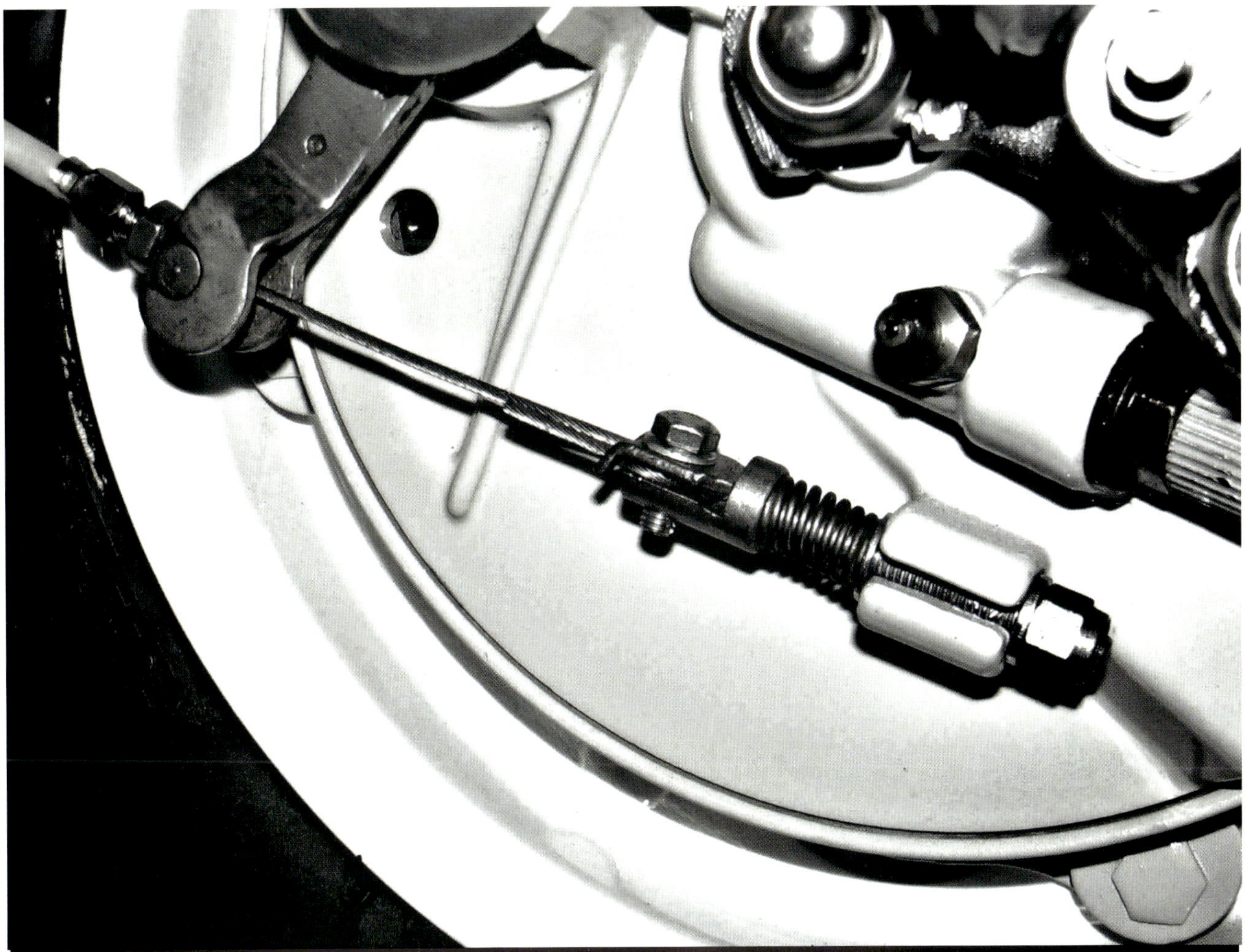

It required drilling the outer cable housing but considerably shortening its length meant more operating pressure could be applied

The improved design had a working prototype fitted to Project 137, the twin-cylinder Lambretta

A solution to get more pressure applied to the disc pad was the reverse-pull system, which was developed at Lambretta Concessionaires. This worked by shortening the cable by over 2ft but meant drilling into the disc back plate to fit it. The other awkward problem was splitting the two halves of the disc for servicing. This was because the disc sat in a recess on the one half but was located on three dowels on the other. Over time, dust from the disc and dirt from the road would result in the disc becoming seized onto the dowels, meaning separating the two halves could be very difficult. Also, the disc had to be free-floating, moving across the dowels as pressure was applied to the moving pad; if it became seized, it made the brake less efficient.

While it was a great invention, there was room to develop it to eliminate the problems highlighted and make it more efficient. When Project 137, the twin-cylinder Lambretta prototype, was created, it also featured a much-improved front disc brake. The disc was now fixed solidly to the left side half, secured by four bolts on its external diameter and doing away with the dowels. The pads were now housed in a separate unit that fitted into the right-hand side in a cassette design. With the fixed disc sitting in between when the cable was moved by the brake arm, the applied pressure was much more substantial. The unit was now held in place by four fixing screws doing away with the circlip and not only making it much more secure but a sealed component.

This proved that the disc was developed, and a working prototype was also produced. In 1967, an extension was added to the homologation certificate for the SX 200 produced in late 1965. This was for the new disc brake design and included its new dimensions and operating mechanism. With it approved, it would be expected to appear on the SX 200 soon afterwards. Yet not only did it not appear on later SX 200 machines, but it was left off the Grand Prix 200 too, and both continued to use the original design. This myth is one that doesn't quite get fully answered in that while it can be proven that it was designed and was ready to go into production, the reason why it only ever appeared on a prototype remains elusive.

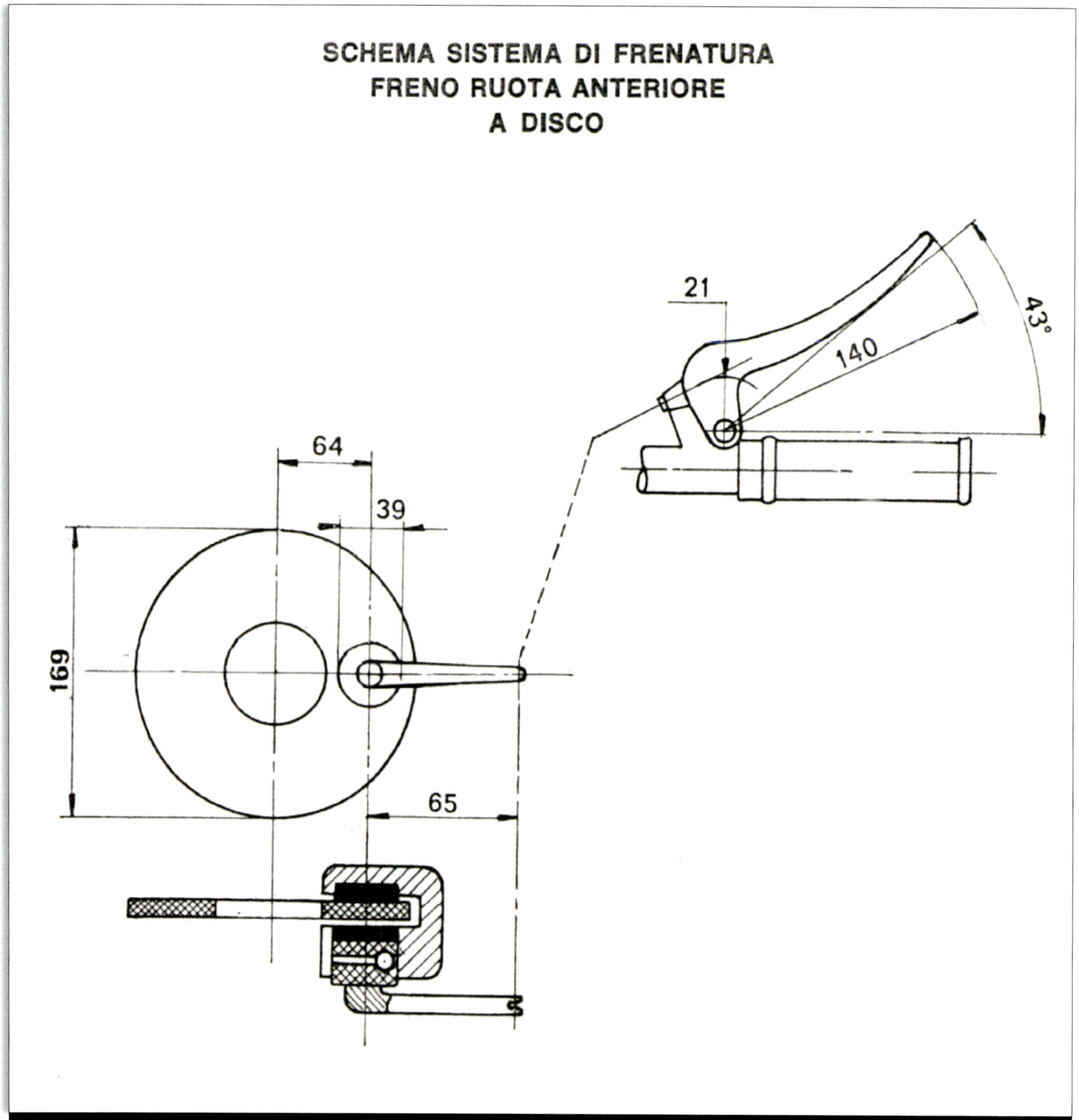

The drawing of the original disc design approved on the SX 200 homologation certificate in October 1965

NOTA - Estensione dell'omologazione n. 4355 OM del 14.10.1965 con certificato n. 5154 OM del 12.6.1967. A partire dal veicolo avente telaio n. **845000** e dalla **dichiarazione** di conformità in data **15-4-1967** in alternativa verrà montato un nuovo gruppo frenante anteriore a disco avente diverso bloccaggio della pinza e del disco secondo lo schema seguente:

γ = 43°

x = 140

y = 21

z = 65

$Ø_1$ DISCO = 200

n = 71

$Ø_2$ PASTIGLIA = 39

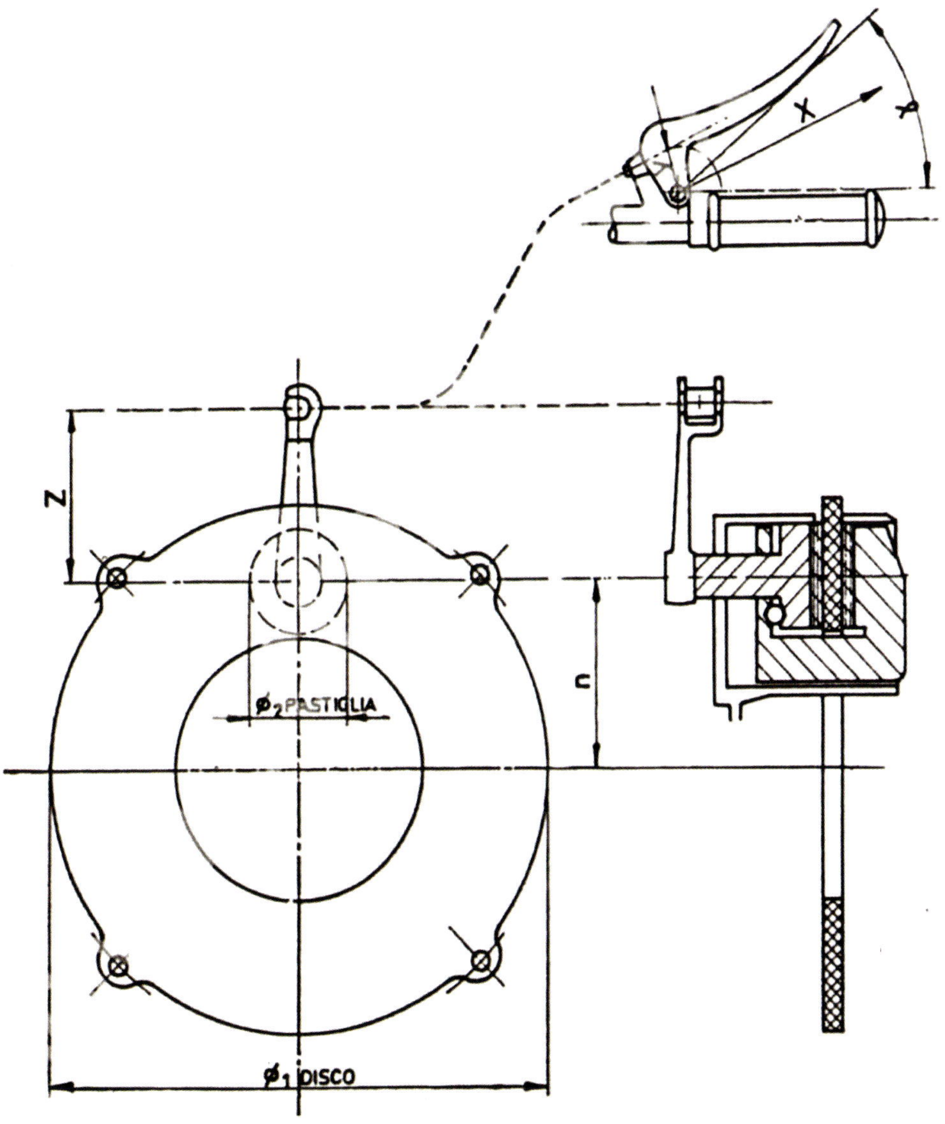

An extension to the homologation certificate for the improved design dated June 12, 1967. It states that from SX 200 frame number 845000, the front disc brake design will be fitted. For some reason, it wasn't

27
Engine continuity

During the 24 years of Lambretta production at the Innocenti factory, more than three million units were produced in total. One of the reasons for the success of the Lambretta was its reliability and, like any vehicle, that centred around the engine. If, for any reason, an engine consistently breaks down, then the reputation of a brand can quickly become tarnished. The Lambretta engine was compact and basic in its design but proved very durable and rarely had any problems. Producing that many machines meant that not only did each engine have to work perfectly, but it also had to have continuity. In other words, each one had to produce the same amount of power to ensure no variation.

That may sound easy but a good example of how difficult that is can be found with Li series three scooters. Between the 125 and 150cc variants, approximately 290,000 were produced over a period of five years. That equates to 1,100 per week, which is a staggering amount, so how was it possible to ensure each one produced the same amount of power? The answer was by testing them, but that couldn't be done once the machine was built; it needed to be carried out before the engine was fitted into the frame. Once each engine was built, it went into a testing bay where it would run for 30 minutes. During that time, its revs were recorded, and the amount of power produced at its peak.

Thirty engines at a time were tested and run on the same fuel, and all were connected to a remote airbox setup, which was identical to those on the machine. Any engine that produced a bhp figure outside the correct figure or failed to get to maximum revs was taken back and checked to be tested again until it worked correctly. This lengthy process showed how committed Innocenti was to making sure each Lambretta performed flawlessly to the exact specifications that were set.

Workers on the engine assembly line putting them together

The engine was run at different rev ranges over 30 minutes to make sure it produced the correct power

28
Li spoked wheels

When introduced in 1958, the new Lambretta Li models were a revelation. Far removed from their shaft-driven predecessors, the Li 125 and 150 were a completely new design. Part of this was the enlarging of the wheel diameter from eight to ten inches. Not only would this improve handling, but it would also allow for a bigger brake surface area.

At the official UK press launch, a photograph was taken of James Agg announcing the new model to the assembled press. A brand-new Li 125 was directly behind him with strange anomalies on the front and rear hub. Both had cutouts representing a four-leaf clover shape, exposing the inner workings of the hub. While it must be presumed this was for demonstration purposes, it has never been explained if this was so or whether it was an intentional part of the design.

The rear hub image blown up shows the hub with a cross-shaped look

The press shot of the Li 125 with James Agg standing in front of it. The cloverleaf cut out on the rear hub is clearly visible; at the front, it is partially visible

Section 2: The Ones That Can't Be Explained

29

The mysterious Grand Prix 150

The UK sales pamphlet for the Grand Prix range looked normal enough

The release of the new Lambretta range in 1969 couldn't come quickly enough as public anticipation of the latest model began to grow. In Italy, it was called the DL, but it was the UK that branded it the Grand Prix. Not only was this a much better-sounding name, but it also suited the engine's performance. All three variants, 125, 150, and 200, were the most powerful Innocenti had created, and the sporting name suggested such. The only cosmetic difference was the badge, and on the 150 model the paint scheme was available in two-tone as opposed to one single colour.

Image three shows a red Grand Prix 150 to the right of the picture

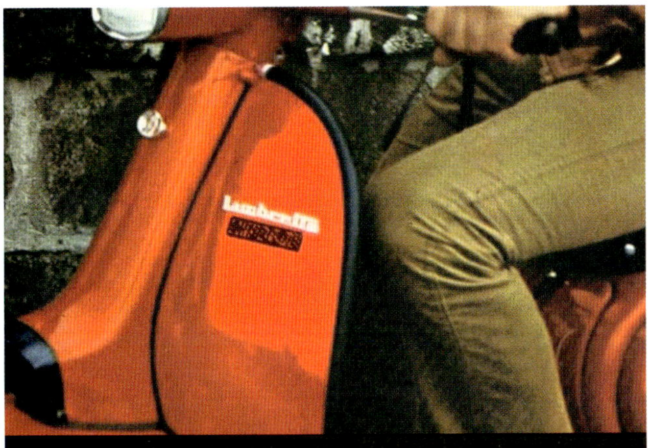
Blown up, the image of the leg shield badges reveals a strange-looking inscription that appears to have been scrawled over

There was very little advertising literature for the new Lambretta, and one reason for this was the scaling back of the advertising budget compared to the earlier years of production. There was an official Italian sales pamphlet where it was labelled as the DL and a UK one with the Grand Prix insignia. What was strange is that the UK-branded Grand Prix featured machines were photographed in Italy rather than being done in the UK. While that may have been due to a lack of time to prepare the photographs for the literature before the official launch, there is a strange anomaly in one of the pictures.

Of the four colour images used on the pamphlet, the third one shows a red Grand Prix on the right. When the image is blown up, it shows the badges on the front leg shields in more detail. There should be an oblong badge underneath the Lambretta script with the inscription 'Grand Prix 150'. Instead, the badge appears almost see-through, with the red paint visible and the inscription scribbled out. No explanation has ever been given as to what the wording was and why the correct badge was not in place.

How the badge should have looked

30
The Pegasus seat

When the TV 175 was introduced in 1957, it had many new features never before seen on a Lambretta – one of them being a dual seat. The lower capacity 125 and 150cc variants were only offered with single saddles, which continued into the series two and three lineups. Advertising always stated that the dual seat on the more powerful model gave added comfort, especially when touring with a pillion passenger, which was a perfectly reasonable claim to make. There was, however, a difference to the dual seat for the UK market that was commonplace from the series two TV 175 onwards.

Instead of the Italian-manufactured dual seat, it used a British-made one called the Pegasus. It had a much lower, flat-looking appearance and, instead of being spring-loaded, had a solid base with foam inner. When the TV 175 series three was launched, all UK examples were fitted with the Pegasus seat throughout its entire availability.

The TV 200 was also equipped with the same seat, but that later changed to the traditional Italian version towards the end of production. While it is accepted that Pegasus seats were fitted on UK versions, there has never been any explanation as to why this is so or why Lambretta Concessionaires discontinued it on the TV 200 later on.

It must be remembered that it required the purchase of vast numbers of seats from the Birmingham-based company, and then each one needed to be fitted. Not only would this mean more labour to carry out the job, but it would also incur an extra cost. Theories regarding why it was used centre around the Pegasus seat being more comfortable, which is the only plausible explanation unless any evidence or official paperwork regarding the decision to use it comes to light.

The UK version of the TV 175 series three in an early press shot showing the much lower shape of the Pegasus seat

Press image showing one fitted in mid-production

Later production models of the TV 200 used the factory standard dual seat shown in this UK advert

The dual-seat version manufactured by Giuliari and Noemi Rosa fitted as factory standard

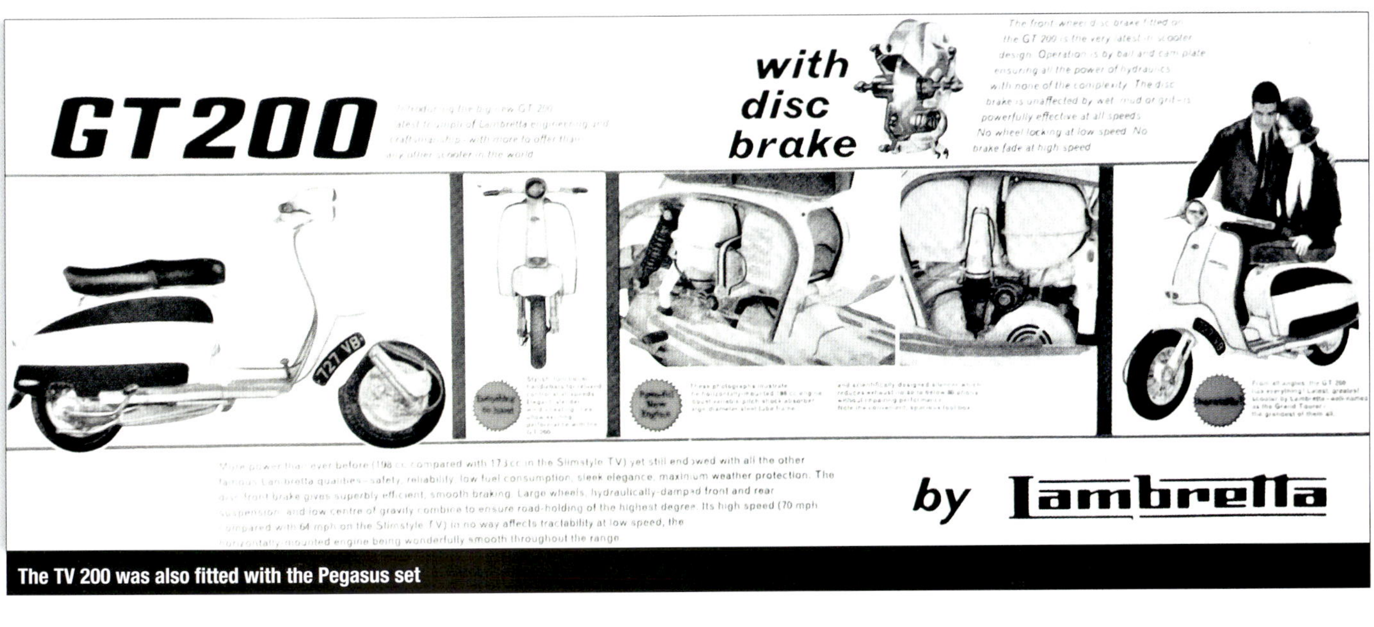

The TV 200 was also fitted with the Pegasus set

31
Painted engine mounts and bolts

When the Lambretta series three Slimstyle was introduced, the most powerful machine at the time was the TV 175. It still used the same engine design as the series two version but featured an upgrade to the engine mounts. Before, it was a short solid rubber-type mount, which now changed to a bigger flexible type. This was to lower engine vibration and to help with engine flex during acceleration. It would be used on the higher capacity models, while the lower capacity ones would retain the solid mount. During the mid-1960s, all Lambretta models would switch to the bigger flexible type mount.

When the TV 175 series three was first introduced, the engine mounts were painted white on the outside around the whole circumference. The reason for doing this was never disclosed, and there seemed no advantage to be gained. The painting of them wasn't continued on future series three models, which had this type of mount fitted and were left in bare metal. When Innocenti stopped painting them, it proved there was no advantage in carrying out the practice, but it doesn't explain why it was done in the first place.

Also painted were the two 7mm bolts that held the removable footboard leg on the kickstart side to allow for the removal of the side case. All series three models, whatever colour was used, had these two bolts painted in that shade. There was no cosmetic reason for doing it, as they were hidden underneath the side panel. Also, once removed to gain access to the side case, the paint on them would be scratched. There is no explanation as to why the bolts were painted and how they were tightened up in the factory without being marked.

The shorter solid mount type used on earlier models

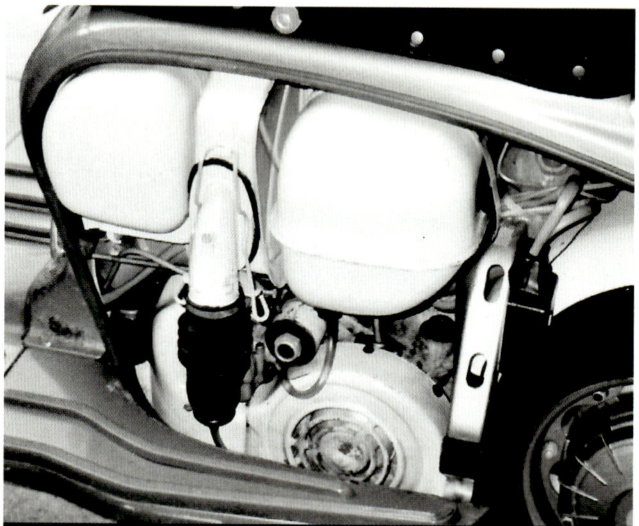
The entire circumference of the mount was painted bright white

The removable mount of the footboard strut had the two 7mm bolts painted in the colour used on the bodywork right up to and including the Grand Prix

It would peel off over time, most likely because it got hot when the engine was running

INNOCENTI Lambretta	Type 175 TV	TECHNICAL INFORMATION	N° 11	SERVICE DEPARTMENT Motor-Scooter
	SECTION: VARIOUS			Date: 16/5/1962

- completely release the control cable from the lever placed on the pads housing, as shown in figure 3;
- slacken the nut using a «crowfoot» type wrench (see figure 4) on the fixed pad side and, acting on the screw inside the nut with a 4 mm Allen wrench, tighten this screw;
- after tightening, rotate back the screw by one turn and lock it by means of the nut. The fixed pad is then locked once again;
- fix again the control cable to the corresponding lever. The cable will be stretched again by means of the adjusting threaded button. Braking should start as soon as the brake lever on the handlebar is operated.

SILENT BLOCK

A new type of silent block has been mounted to reduce the vibrations transmitted by the engine to the frame (see the figures herebelow).

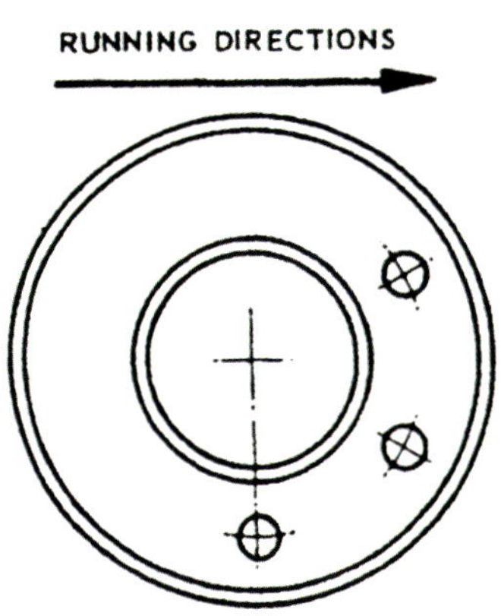

Fig. 5

Fig. 6

Therefore, all the vibrations are reduced with this new model, in particular at high speeds. The coupling pin fixing the engine to the frame has been lenthened and the silent blocks have been overhanged in relation to the engine holding lugs.

It should be noticed that three holes have been made in the rubber of the new silent block. These holes modify the flexible coupling behaviour.

Therefore, the silent block should be assembled with a well determined orientation. In fact, one hole should be turned downwards, while the two others should face the front part of the vehicle.

Introduced on the TV 175 series three, the much larger flexible rubber engine mount

32
TV 200 red tape

The story about the TV 200 and its export-only status is common knowledge. Most were sent to the UK as per the deal with Lambretta Concessionaires, with a few examples going to other parts of the world just before production ended. While the mysteries surrounding its production have been cleared up, one thing hasn't been explained. On the fork stem between the bracket where the horn casting bolts to and the top of the headset, a piece of red tape was put around the circumference of the tube during production.

This wasn't noticed until the 1980s when original examples were being restored for the first time, and the tape was exposed when the machine was taken apart. Although it was something very simple, which would have taken only a matter of seconds to do, why was it being done at all? It has been suggested that it enabled workers on the production line to identify it as a TV 200, indicating to them that only certain parts would fit it. This theory doesn't stand up however because, apart from the engine, nothing was different compared to a TV 175. At the time, as well as the TV models, several others were being built, such as the Li 125, 150, and Li 150 Special, and all had differences in their engines, bodywork and badges, but they didn't have an identifying mark like this on them.

It has also been suggested that it may have had something to do with not requiring homologation and being an export model. The problem with this theory is that the tape was not visible once each machine was built up, so it couldn't be used as an identifying mark. Some unrestored examples don't have the tape present, but it is possible that over the course of many intervening years it had either fallen off or been removed when the cables were being serviced. Regardless, there have been many examples of it being present, so it isn't a one-off. The reason for it being there must have been to do with part of the production process and identify the frame, but why and for what purpose has never been adequately proven or explained.

Three different examples of unrestored TV 200 frames that all have the red piece of tape on the fork stem

33
Was the design of the Grand Prix influenced by the UK

Production of the new DL Lambretta began in January 1969, having been approved for homologation in Italy in October 1968. The new design still used the existing dimensions of the series three range, albeit with a few modifications. The Bertone team, tasked with the design, took the existing SX model and, with a few subtle changes, produced a stunning and modern-looking machine. While it is accepted that Bertone made the changes, were they influenced by designs in the UK that preceded what they did?

Two distinctive modifications were made to the Lambretta in 1966 and early 1967 which may have given Bertone ideas. The first was an accessory produced by Arthur Francis of Watford, known as the Cibie headlight. This was a headset conversion for an existing series three which was rectangular instead of the standard round shape. It was photographed on a Lambretta SX 200, and though larger in appearance than the one that would be used on the Grand Prix, it gave an idea of what it would look like.

A few months later Supertune Ltd, a Lambretta-based shop in Croydon, showcased a machine called the Lowline, where a TV 200 had 3.5 inches taken out of the fork stem to shorten the front end. This was revealed in Practical Scooter, dated September 1967. The modification was based around a tuned sports scooter and made it impractical for road use as the riding position was rather uncomfortable. However, it showed what was possible, and though the GP was only lowered by just under one inch, the basic idea may have come from this design.

Both the lowering of the front end and the rectangular headlamp conversion fit well within the timeframe for

Derek Cook tests the latest —
'LOW LINE SPECIAL FROM SUPERTUNE'

A single racing type seat was fitted which meant that you had to sit right back and crouch, to be comfortable. At high speeds this proved useful.

The bucket seat itself was held by a single hinge at the back to allow the seat to be lifted for fueling. The seat itself was rather uncomfortable.

18 Practical Scooter, September, 1967

Shown in the September 1967 edition of *Practical Scooter* magazine, the Supertune Lowline Special. Though much lower at the front than the Grand Prix, this is the first time this type of modification was seen on a Lambretta and could have influenced the design

The Arthur Francis Cibie headlight conversion shown on an SX 200 in 1966. Though much larger than the one that appeared on the Grand Prix, it does have a similar look about it

The Lowline Special still exists; could it have been the reason for altering the height of the DL?

this theory. The only problem with proving it is the only person who could confirm its truth or otherwise would have been Nuccio Bertone himself, but sadly he is no longer alive. While there can be no definitive answer as to whether these two UK-based modifications influenced the design of the Grand Prix, the possibility can't be ruled out.

One other strange anomaly appeared in 1966 and, for whatever reason, may have also been involved in the rebranding of the DL to the Grand Prix. Peter Agg rebranded the DL as the Grand Prix just has he had done with the TV 200, calling that the GT 200 and calling the Li 150 Special the Pacemaker. Agg was heavily involved with sports car production by way of the Elva and working with Bruce McLaren. He intended to create a Formula One team, which he eventually did in the 1970s and stated that this was the main reason for rebranding the DL as the Grand Prix.

In April 1966, just after the SX 200 was launched in the UK, a report named the new machine the SX Grand Prix 200. There had been no other reports referring to it as such and this left only two possible answers. Firstly, was it something dreamt up by the magazine? That would seem a bit strange as that wouldn't be accurate reporting. The other explanation is that maybe Peter Agg wanted to rebrand the SX 200 as the Grand Prix. The report in the article mentions a quote from Maurice Knight, who was the sales manager of Lambretta Concessionaires, so it is plausible that the magazine got the information directly from a company source. Also, because the last two models introduced in the UK had been rebranded, it seemed that the SX 200 would naturally follow suit. Officially, it was only ever called the SX 200, but there is evidence to suggest that the intention had been to name it the Grand Prix, which in the end happened with the DL.

April, 1966

NEW SX.200.GP LAMBRETTA

0-110 yds in 8.8 secs

Shown in our photograph alongside is the latest Lambretta scooter, built specially for the UK market but intended for later world sales.

Developed by Innocenti from the GT.200 introduced in 1963 this latest, known as the Lambretta SX Grand Prix 200 has a 198cc two-stroke engine, four speed gearbox, disc brakes, dual seat and a 90mph speedo. Time from a standing start to 110 yards is claimed to be an astonishing 8.8secs.

Available in eight colours on basic white the SX Grand Prix 200 costs £216.

Said Lambretta Concessionaries Ltd. Sales manager Maurice Knight: "The success of its predecessor, the GT.200, has shown that the market for machines of this capacity is widening daily.

I have just ridden one of the new models which, although it had only one mile on the clock, impressed me with the smoothness of its acceleration, its latent zest and power, and its quite exceptional road-holding qualities.

The press release that mentions the SX 200 being called the Grand Prix. Is this the model the name was intended to be used on?

Did you know

Lambretta Concessionaires were so successful with their marketing strategy that they had cornered 70% of the scooter market in the UK by 1960. While the Vespa made up most of the remaining figure, other manufacturers were also attempting to gain a sales foothold. Four years earlier, in 1956, 32 companies had been either importing scooters into the country or producing them within the UK – indicating just how congested the marketplace was. By the time production finished at Innocenti in 1971, Lambretta Concessionaires had imported and sold over one million machines, approximately one-third of the Lambrettas produced in Italy.

The demand was so great that up to 10,000 machines a month came into the country, the majority having made most of their journey by rail. The organisation was so good that the unloading was done by a small team of just four men. Despite this, there was a problem with the keys in the early days. Each model had two sets, one for the steering lock and one for the toolbox, with a spare for each. These were tied to the handlebars by a piece of string, and problems arose with them failing off, meaning a considerable amount of time was spent trying to put them back with the machine they had come off. This problem was finally solved simply by putting the keys in the toolbox.

While advertising was a significant part of convincing the customer to buy a Lambretta, the company also made many statements that buying one was a sensible choice. It was stated that because the Lambretta had a two-stroke engine, it had a big advantage over a four-stroke one. These included being mechanically more reliable, getting more miles to the gallon, climbing hills more easily, and carrying two people without much strain on the engine. It was also stated that the two-stroke engine allowed for a much sleeker and more stylish design. Another claim was that because the Lambretta had better weather protection, passengers could ride one in what they labelled 'normal clothes', including the pillion passenger.

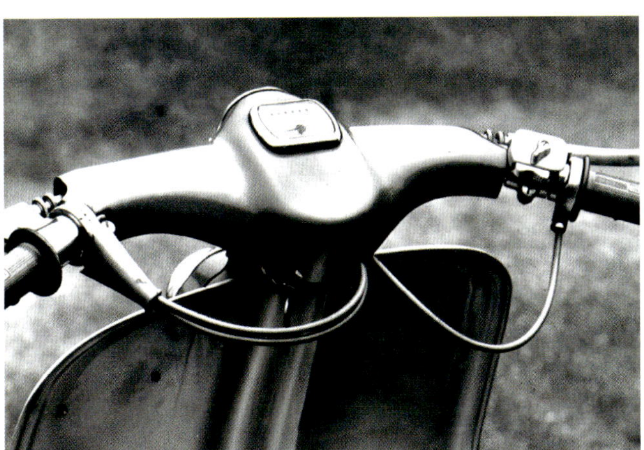

The LD didn't have many keys, but those that did were often lost in the early days

To convince the customer even more, emphasis was placed on the cheapness of spares, meaning repair costs were significantly lower than with rival manufacturers' machines. Also, because so many were on the road, insurance companies would offer more affordable insurance premiums. Safety was also targeted, with it being pointing out that the rider had better protection in the event of an accident. This was a bold claim as there was certainly no guarantee you wouldn't be injured if you fell off. The most absurd statement was that the weather protection was so good, if it was raining, you would be drier taking a journey on a Lambretta than if you had been walking instead. In a similar vein, customers were reminded that a Lambretta was far

Even by the early 1960s, Lambretta was still selling in huge quantities, here are enough machines to keep the company going for about a week

Lambretta Concessionaires always used models from local agencies to advertise the Lambretta

Cables Lambretta London

Lambretta

Lambretta Concessionaires Limited

HEAD OFFICE & SALES ● 424/426 KINGSTON ROAD, RAYNES PARK S.W.20 ● Tel. CHErrywood 3204 (5 lines)
SERVICE STATION ● 213/219 THE BROADWAY, WIMBLEDON S.W.19 ● Tel. LIBerty 7631 (3 lines)
STORES & ACCESSORIES ● 221/227 THE BROADWAY, WIMBLEDON S.W.19 ● Tel. CHErrywood 8232 (2 lines)

TO ALL LAMBRETTA AGENTS.

S A L E S

Remember this, therefore, when you are considering your policy for the 1957 Season and remember too that Lambretta shows a 16% nett return as opposed to its nearest rival at only 13% (from figures kindly supplied by a dealer), together with the fact that Lambretta has now built up an organisation with pioneer experience which has overcome most of the teething troubles prevalent in all new industries - and so successfully conquered these early difficulties that many are now trying to copy our methods even so far as to using our advertising slogans, i.e. "the world's finest scooter", "the Rolls Royce of Scooters", and to using not only our colours but, even now, our price!

Lambretta has the largest scooter production in the world, the million mark having long since been passed, and most important of all for you, the dealer, Lambretta in the U.K. have now sold this year more than all makes of scooters and motorcycles in their classification. We hardly need persuade you, therefore, that you should CONCENTRATE ON WHAT'S BETTER AND SELL LAMBRETTA.

10th July, 1956.

Lambretta Concessionaires were proud of their sales record and were keen to remind dealers constantly

cleaner than a motorcycle, and there was no chance of getting dirty from an oily chain or covered in grease, which, to a certain extent, was true.

To prove the engine's reliability, Lambretta Concessionaires claimed that it could be revved to its maximum and that it thrived on this. They were happy to give a figure of up to 75,000 miles before the engine would need a rebore, even if it had been driven hard, pointing out that no four-stroke machine could offer such reliability. Dealers were regularly updated about why a Lambretta was so good and were instructed to make sure their salesmen constantly reminded potential customers of the quotes. To make sure the salesmen did their job, incentives were given out by way of extra commission if a certain number of machines were sold. To push them even more, there were regular salesman-of-the-month awards with prizes including a car, television and cash. This not only proved to be a popular scheme, but it meant many more machines were being sold because of the rewards the top salesmen would get in return.

Advertising was carried out in all forms of the press, but hundreds of different sales leaflets were produced as well as literature for all models, which could be handed out to the customer. Innocenti produced a great deal of them, while others were done directly in the UK, the work initially being farmed out to agencies to create what was required.

Many different slogans were invented, such as "Travel around better get a Lambretta", "Join the Jet-Set on a Lambretta", and "Lambretta gives you SX appeal", amongst many others. When Bob Wilkinson became advertising manager in the 1960s, he was given a free hand to create the material used. All of the people depicted in this material were models from local agencies in London and, later, some of the rising stars within the ranks of the UK Lambretta scene, especially those who raced.

Bob also decided to include himself in many of the images used, and while he was noticeable in most of them, he sometimes appeared in the background. In one

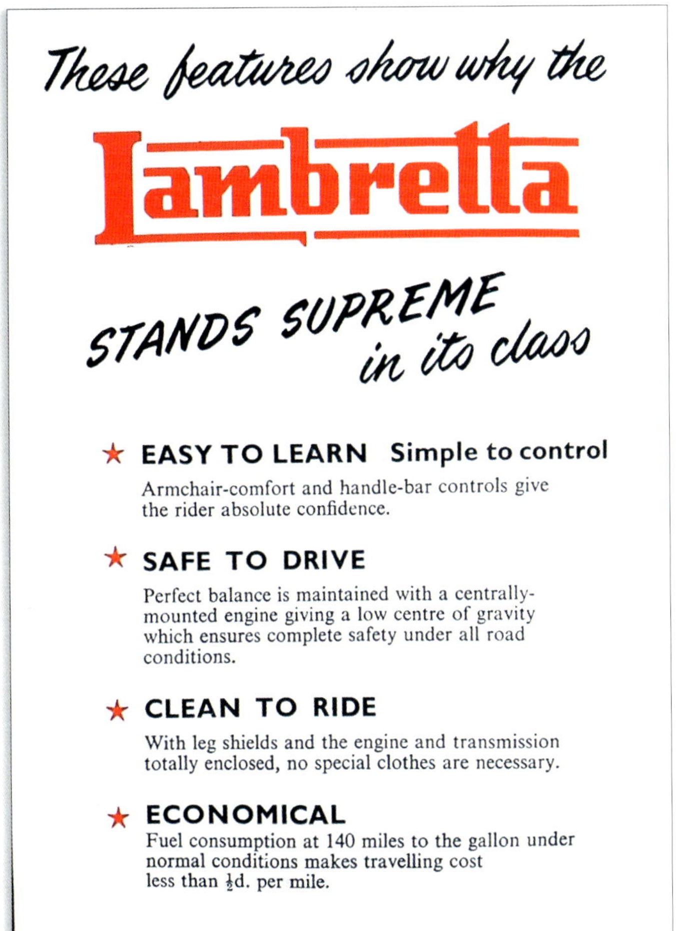

Claims made about how good the Lambretta was were sometimes a bit over the top when trying to convince the public to buy one

One of the most iconic adverts created by Bob Wilkinson, who is seen here at the back of the plane wearing a hat

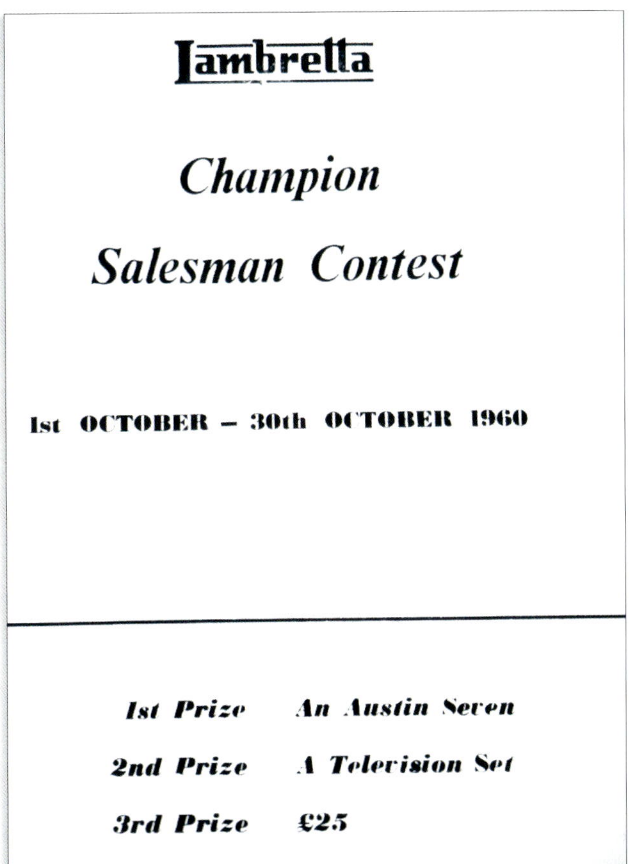
Lambretta

Champion

Salesman Contest

1st OCTOBER – 30th OCTOBER 1960

1st Prize	*An Austin Seven*
2nd Prize	*A Television Set*
3rd Prize	*£25*

Incentives for salesmen to sell more machines were rewarding at the time

Lambretta (AUSTRALASIA) PTY. LTD.
22 WA[illegible] STREET, ARTARMON N.S.W. 2054, AUSTRALIA
TELEPHONE 439 [illegible], 439-1920, 439-[illegible]
Telegrams & Cables: LAMSEC, SYDNEY.

Lambretta

NEWS RELEASE

No.1.

<u>FOR IMMEDIATE RELEASE</u> May, 1969

<u>HALF-MILLION DOLLAR SCOOTER COMEBACK</u>

Lambretta is about to stage a $500,000 comeback on the Australian two-wheel market.

A pilot shipment of the latest model scooters arrived in Sydney this week.

Additional consignments totalling 700 are in transit from Milan, Italy.

Lambretta (Australasia) Pty. Ltd. will soon launch a major advertising and promotional campaign to re-establish the brand.

The company is a subsidiary of the multi-million dollar Lambretta Trojan Group of Surrey, England, and is the wholesale distributor for Australia, Papua and New Guinea, New Zealand, the Solomon Islands, Fiji, Tahiti, Noumea and Hawaii.

Headquartered at Artarmon, Sydney, Lambretta Australasia will use its 12,000 square foot plant as a stock holding depot, main parts store, and dealer training depot.

Initially, four models will be offered. Prices range from under $300.00 to $550.00

The ill-fated attempt to beat the crippling taxes in the UK by setting up a concession in Australia which lasted a matter of months

The Grand Prix was so liked by the public that it allowed the company to buck the trend of declining UK sales of two-wheeled machines. If the Lambretta had not been culled by Leyland Innocenti, then most likely, it would have survived like the Vespa did

iconic advert, featuring the SX 200 at Gatwick airport, Bob is in the background carrying luggage from a plane and wearing a trilby hat as a sort of disguise.

In the latter part of the 1960s, the UK economy was in dire trouble, and the devaluation of the pound was the final straw for Lambretta Concessionaires. Devaluation not only raised the price of a Lambretta significantly, because it was imported, but also resulted in constant increases in purchase tax. Fed up with earning less profit because of failed government policies, Lambretta Concessionaires devised a bold plan to set up Lambretta importation into Australia. That had been happening since the late 1940s, but the idea was to take over running it by getting the licence from Innocenti to do so. This outraged the Australian importers, but the bold claims that many more Lambrettas would be sold through the new company persuaded Innocenti to go with them instead.

The set-up cost was huge, and several top people at the Lambretta Concessionaires were sent over to run the company. However, the lack of research and the fact that the Lambretta wasn't ideally suited to much of

As the 1960s progressed, they exploited the sexual revolution as far as they dared

Many slogans were created that were catchy and easy to remember

the rough terrain and long roads meant it was doomed to failure from the outset. Within six months, the company was shut down due to losing so much money, and while there was a blame game going on, it showed that the Lambretta did have its drawbacks in certain environments. The aftermath meant the only option was to continue selling the Lambretta in the UK, and this gave those in charge a new impetus to buck the trend of declining sales of two-wheeled vehicles.

Thanks to the introduction of the Grand Prix, they managed to do this by working hard and having such a stunning design. For the next two years, sales figures of the Lambretta rose considerably and the future looked bright. Sadly, that was curtailed when production of the Lambretta finished in 1971, which was a shame because there was no denying the company had the right people to ensure it could have continued. If the rash decision to cull the Lambretta so abruptly had not happened, most likely, it would still be in production today.

Facts and figures

The biggest selling Lambretta ever was the Li 150 series two, with approximately 162,000 being produced

The biggest selling range was the Li series three, with a total of 288,000 units made

The SX 200 was the first Lambretta to feature a 90mph speedometer

TV 200
Maximum power: 10.75 bhp
Peak Power: 5700 rpm
Fourth gear ratio: 4.45
Speed at peak power: 65mph
Revs at claimed top speed: 5800 = 66mph
Revs required to reach 70mph: 6200
Acceleration – Quarter mile time: N/A
Percentage rise between gears: 39/37/30
Power to weight ratio: 0.0874HP per 1kg

SX 200
Maximum power:11.00 bhp
Peak Power: 5500rpm
Fourth gear ratio: 4.82
Speed at peak power: 58mph
Revs at claimed top speed: 6300 = 66mph
Revs required to reach 70mph: 6700
Acceleration – Quarter mile time: 23.2 seconds
Percentage rise between gears: 43,39,31
Power to weight ratio: 0.0894HP per 1kg

GP 200
Maximum power:11.74 bhp
Peak Power: 6200rpm
Fourth gear ratio: 5.22
Speed at peak power: 60 mph
Revs at claimed top speed: 7100 = 69mph
Revs required to reach 70mph: 7200rpm
Acceleration – Quarter mile time: 21.1 seconds
Percentage rise between gears: 43,35,30
Power to weight ratio: 0.108HP per 1kg

Over half a million series three large frame machines were produced in total, but the 200cc models only made up 8.5% of that figure

The most expensive Lambretta to purchase was the Grand Prix 200 Electronic, costing £271 in the spring of 1971

The SX 150 was the only Lambretta outside of the Grand Prix range to be painted in more than one colour by the factory, available in green and orange

The plastic toolbox, slot-in fork rubbers and clip-on side panels associated with the Grand Prix were introduced during very late SX production

The first dual seat on a Lambretta was introduced on the TV 175 series one in 1957

The most powerful 200cc Lambretta was the Grand Prix 200, which produced 11.74bhp

The fibreglass front mudguard was first used on the TV 175 series three, followed by the TV 200 and Li 150 Special

The DL had what was known as the 'ink splat' logo on the right-hand side of the leg shields, while the Grand Prix had a chequered flag.

The 'Rallymaster', based on an Li 150 series two, was technically the only ever sports Lambretta and one to feature a tuned engine

The SX 200 had an elongated kickstart pedal unique to this model

The Li 150 series three ran for the longest production time of any Lambretta, totalling five years and five months

The most powerful 150cc Lambretta produced was shared by the SX and Grand Prix 150, both producing 9.4bhp

The first Lambretta to have dampers fitted on the front forks was the TV 175 series one

The SX 200 was the only 200cc Lambretta to feature its capacity on a side panel badge

Every Lambretta model produced by Innocenti was fitted with a Dellorto carburettor

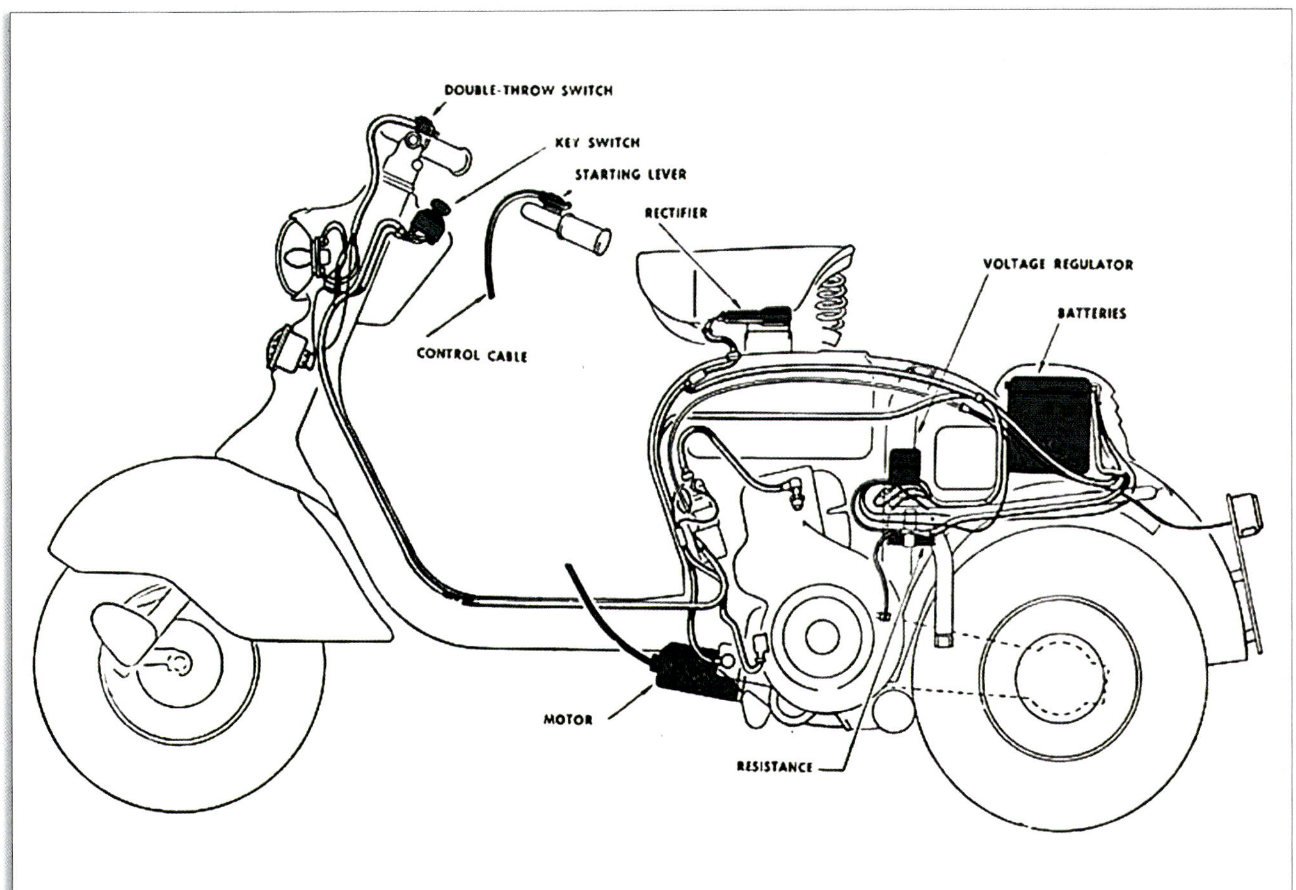

The LD was the only Lambretta to be fitted with an electric start system

The LC 125, which started production in April 1950, was the first Lambretta to feature side panels